Westray Baptist Church

1810 – 2010

A View from the Pew

God Bless

Margaret A. Scott

Dedication

For Jack, who knew so much more of this history, and who made some of it himself.

Westray Baptist Church

1810 – 2010

A View from the Pew

Margaret A. Scott

Published by

Information Plus,
3 Hill of Heddle
Finstown,
Orkney.
KW17 2LH

www.information-plus.co.uk

Copyright © Margaret A. Scott 2010

Front cover by Julie Hagan

(For details of photos see page 103)

Original drawing by Catherine A. S. Stevenson

Printed by:

The Orcadian, Hell's Half Acre, Kirkwall

ISBN   978-0-9554644-0-9

Contents

Introduction

When someone reaches a special birthday it is time to look back at origins, mull over experiences, enjoy the present, have a party and look forward to what may be in store for the future.

Westray Baptist Church has reached its two hundredth birthday and that is something to give thanks to God for and to celebrate. There is a long list of names of faithful people who have supported the church during the years. It would be impossible to record them here but they will all appear in the Lamb's book of Life.

Perhaps someone sometime will be able to write a more complete history of the two hundred years of Baptist witness in Westray but on this occasion a more concise research and a collection of memories may be more acceptable.

Personally I have known about the church for nigh on eighty years. I was a member for forty years and was married to its secretary, John Scott, who was in office continually for forty three years. I wish he had been here to help with this collection of facts and figures. I continue to have a prayerful interest in it with my son-in-law, Stephen Hagan, now the present secretary.

Thank you to all those who have contributed and encouraged me in producing this collection of memories, photos and reflections. Please excuse any inaccuracies from whatever source.

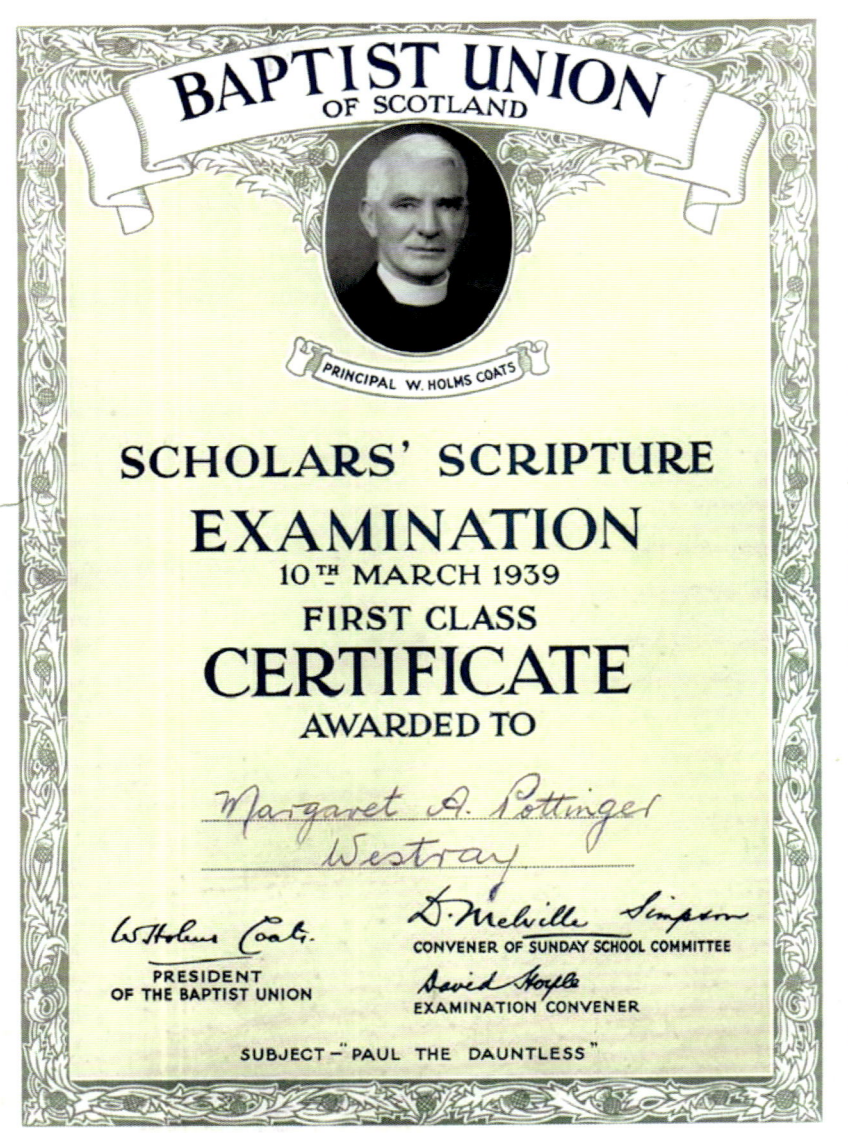

This certificate was presented to the author over 70 years ago after her Sunday school studies with Miss Balfour - it maybe qualifies her to present this history!

A Brief History

1810-1860

Proper church minutes for the first hundred years are regrettably non-existent but one can piece a lot of the story together from the further reading found at the end of this book. To me it was very exciting to find an old magazine called, "*The Evangelist*" when we emptied the house at Belltowers. This was a periodical published from 1846 until 1853 and it had been subscribed to by John Swanney who had lived there. In it was the obituary of Janet Reid of Breckowall 1784 -1846. It is well worth a read as it tells how people were now reading the Bible for themselves and finally coming to the realisation that baptism by immersion was for them. She was excited about how the Lord provided buildings to worship in, the Tabernacle in the north end of the island and the East Chapel further south. In 1803 the four biggest landowners refused to let the young church have land to build on but Jerome Rendall of Breckaskaill sold them a suitable site and also let them have timber all at a reasonable price.

She and her husband John were of one mind when it came to being baptised and to support the newly formed Baptist Church. Both were Reids and born in Westray. John was the second of two sons born to William Reid and Marjory Rendall, and she was one of five children born to another William Reid and Catherine Rendall. She also went on to be supportive of missionary work in this country and abroad.

On John's death certificate he is said to be a landed proprietor. It could be that he made his fortune outside of Orkney but his generosity benefited the Baptist church as he provided first a manse for the minister, and then a park on which to build a church. This was completed in 1850.

It is also a source of information to read The Trust Deed for the settlement of John Reid's affairs after his decease. Much of his estate was left to the Westray Strict Baptist Church although relatives and friends are not forgotten. The trustees are named as the two young ministers of the church, Rev Henry Harcus and Rev James Scott, all the deacons at the time and those that would follow them. Both Henry Harcus and James Scott refrained from acting as trustees. The document gives us the names of the deacons of which otherwise we would have been ignorant. John Reid died in 1865 thus the information that we have of the Reids gives us a picture of the first fifty years of the life of the church.

1860-1910

During the second half of the nineteenth century the population in Westray was at its highest, remaining about the 2000 mark. At the same time however nearly 1600 people had migrated most of them going to America, like Rev. Henry Harcus. His departure marked the end of long pastorates for the time being. Mr Tulloch's had extended to fifty five years and he died in 1858. Mr Harcus had been the pastor for twenty eight years.

Soon after this, in the sixties, came times of revival when many were baptised and the church membership grew. About 1866 a student from Spurgeon's College came to Westray and was befriended by Henry Harcus and his son-in-law, also a student of the same college. They allowed him to preach and too late they realised that he was of the Christian Brethren persuasion. The result was two thirds of the membership left the church and began holding meetings in a nearby hall.

After 'the split' Mr Gavin Mowat came from Shetland to encourage the remaining members. In 1870 the Rev George Macdonald, from the Home Mission, took charge for five years. The work again prospered under his devoted leadership. The ministers that followed were Rev J.A. Marnie, two years, Rev P.F. Slater thirteen years and Rev J Yeomans, five years. During these years migration continued and the island population began to fall. Baptist Church membership remained about the same as it had been after the split. However, as a result of a mission by Mr A.Y. McGregor in the winter of 1903-04, fifty people were baptised and joined the church. The Rev Albert Griffiths was the minister at the time. Revival blessing continued and in 1908 the Rev W.C. Charteris writes that twenty two names were added to the roll. During his time a hall was added to the church building. This was used for prayer meetings and on Sunday, a Bible Class for the young people, while the Sunday School met in the church itself. The Rev William Gilmour was the minister when the church celebrated its centenary in 1910. Meetings were held to mark the occasion and special speakers were Rev Percival Waugh, Edinburgh and Rev J.A. Grant of Perth. The minister from Burray Baptist Church and other local ministers took part also.

1910 -1960

In 1912 an evangelistic mission was conducted by Mr J.G. Smith of the Gordon Mission, Aberdeen. Just before the First World War a time of great blessing was experienced in the church and eighteen people were baptised.

A Burray minister, Mr Edward Hogg, was called to Westray in 1916. He is remembered for his musical abilities. In 1919 shortly after the Armistice the Rev Joseph Burns held an evangelistic mission when Christians were quickened and also many young people converted. Soon afterwards twenty three people were added to the roll bringing it back to its pre-war strength.

Following Mr Hogg's ministry there were two ministries of fifteen and sixteen years. Rev John Lawrie who came first is remembered as a good visitor who walked many miles. The Christian Endeavour, Bible Class and Sunday School flourished under his leadership. Cottage meetings in the remote districts continued as they had done in previous years. The same ministry pattern continued in Rev James Pottinger's time. There was a war going on which made some differences.

After the Armistice there followed many evangelistic campaigns and many were baptised and entered membership. 1954 saw some Baptist families leave the island to settle mainly in Kirkwall where they, with help from the mother church, founded another Baptist church thus answering the prayers of Mr Pottinger and others.

Secondary schoolchildren from Westray who had to attend Kirkwall Grammar School also had a spiritual home from home.

1960 -2010

Since 1960 shorter ministries have been more common. Rev Brydon Maben stayed for three years and accomplished a lot in that time. He gathered a choir of more than thirty men from all the denominations on the island and some from Kirkwall as well. As the "Men of Orkney" they travelled extensively and he gave members encouragement to testify at meetings and often gave an address himself. The women were not forgotten as he supported Betty when she introduced Women's Auxiliary to the church. This was Brydon's first church. He left to go to College and then joined the Church of Scotland.

Of the next four ministries three were also firsts.

The Rev Henry Telfer 1963-70 from London Bible College, the Rev Raymond Thomson 1971-77 from the Irish Baptist College, the Rev Foster Wright 1977 – 1983 from a former pastorate and Rev Jim Miller 1983 – 1989 from Scottish Baptist College ministered for just over twenty five years in total. Those four young men worked diligently for the extension of God's Kingdom. They showed wisdom in the way they accepted the island situation and as a result there were no discords in the fellowship. The school chaplaincy, started in Mr Pottinger's time, continued until about 1980. The church roll remained about the same level as previously in spite of several young people leaving the island for education and then settling in the south. Many of them became active in churches there.

Archie McColl came to Westray from Cumbernauld in1990 and Hugh McConnachie came from the Scottish Baptist College in 1996 where he had taken a course to fit him for the ministry following his working life in industry. Steve Langford came from Bristol Baptist College in 2002.

Present day

Today the visitor to Westray can see Noltland Castle as it was in 1803 when the first dissenting group worshipped in its hall. He can see the house, known as the Vestry, built on the site of the Tabernacle, the house known as the East Chapel which looks nearly the same as it did in 1839, and he can visit St Mary's churchyard and see the burial places of William Tulloch, James Scott and other co pastors and leaders' families. Finally the visitors will get a welcome at the present church which is in good repair although a major modernisation is in the pipeline. A number of folk now attend the fellowship after the closure of the Westray U F church and other members and adherents have moved to the island. When you add to that the fact that a new young minister has just been inducted and will stay in a fine modern manse, Bellavista up at the Braehead, it augurs well for the future of the Westray Baptist Church as it enters another century.

Westray Baptist Church, also known locally as the Baptist Kirk or the Chapel

Inside the Kirk looking towards the congregation (above)
and towards the pulpit (below)

A Memoir of Janet Reid Breckowall

The subject of the following sketch was born in 1784, in Westray, Orkney. She was the oldest of five children, and was brought up strictly under her father's roof, he being a deacon of the church. The date of her first religious impressions appears to have been about the year 1803, when Mr William Tulloch preached several times in Westray.

From her own account of the origin of the church, we obtain the following particulars "The first time Mr and Mrs Tulloch came to Westray they had to put back again, and it was two weeks before the weather permitted them to come. I considered that a long time, for in the interval my mind was more fully awakened than it was when he was in the place. The feelings that I had when I heard him were nearly worn off again; but one Sabbath, in the latter end of harvest, being at the parish, the precentor read a sermon, which he had permission from the minister to do. A sentence caught my attention as I thought, but I know not if there is such a question in any book: it was this: 'You may as well say there is an honest thief as a prayerless Christian.' I immediately saw, that whilst I lived prayerless I was not a Christian, and, of course, could not have a hope of eternal life. I said nothing, but lived in the full expectation that when Mr Tulloch came, he would teach me all that I needed to know. And truly it was from him that I first learned what to believe and what to obey."

From another account given by herself, she says, " When the eyes of my understanding were enlightened I found that I was a *depraved sinner*; but when I saw that Jesus Christ was born to *save sinners* from their sins, and that he was pointed at as the Lamb of God which taketh away the sin of the world, and that he said himself, 'Come onto me, all ye that labour and are heavy laden, and I will give you rest,' I hasted and fled to Jesus with all my sins. I fled to him for pardon, justification, sanctification, adoption, and comfort, and that I might be glorified with him; for without him I can do nothing, and with him I enjoy all things."

Mrs Reid was one of the first fifteen Dissenters and Independents in the island, and one of the first to be baptised in obedience to her Saviour. With reference to this change in sentiment, she says, "When the subject of believers' baptism arose, some considered it the path of duty at the first hearing, and some did not. It was a matter of private inquiry a good while. The very first time that I heard of it, my heart warmed to it; and ever after I found it a most agreeable subject, because I found it agreeable to the scriptures. But when the opposite view was started, especially from those that I esteemed better than myself, my heart would sink in me like cold lead, and chiefly when it came from my beloved Pastor. Too much respect for him held me in the dark much longer than I might have been. Sometimes I would be afraid to believe that I was right and he wrong, and was under a bondage to open my mouth to scarce any individual, in case of being suspected of heresy. But my partner says he never once doubted it when once he believed it; neither would I, if our Pastor had not appealed to his learning, which made many of us believe that he saw things in the scriptures that we could not see, because we were unlearned."

About this time, Mr Mackay, from Caithness, happened to be in Kirkwall, and hearing that the Independent Church in Westray had changed their views, came over to see, and baptised seven men the day after, among whom was the Pastor himself, who, shortly after, baptised Mrs Reid and several others. At this time she endured heavy persecutions, but this did not daunt her. She steadily persevered in her Christian course, and ever maintained a walk and conversation becoming the gospel. She was the humble means of leading many to the house of prayer, and, among the rest, him who became the partner of her life. She mourned over the wickedness and carelessness of her neighbours, and, together with her husband, liberally supported the gospel in the locality where her lot was cast. She ever manifested great delight in the progress of the Lord's work, and made herself familiar with missionary detail, which never failed to cheer and enliven her mind.

For the last four years of her life she was, through severe affliction, closely confined to her bed, which led her to reflect on the Lord's dealings with her; and although sadly tried and distressed at having to be absent from the means of grace, she ever manifested patient acquiescence in the will of her Heavenly Father. She still however could enjoy epistolary correspondence with Christian friends; and many of her letters are deeply interesting, and breathe a devotional frame of mind in a very high degree.

In her letters she often expressed a great abhorrence of pride; and anything like extravagance in a Christian she loudly condemned. In these particulars she was a truly worthy example; and, owing to the simplicity of her habits, expressed her surprise how a follower of Jesus could use silver articles, when inferior ones might answer the same purpose as well; and her reason for this was, "that their worth might be given to the cause of God." She boldly and earnestly contended for the faith once delivered to the saints. This led her to lament over the low state of the Baptist denomination especially in her own islands; and when the Baptist Union was formed, she wrote to one of the secretaries, how much her heart rejoiced and lifted up, because one of their plans was to "visit every town and city in Scotland, preaching the faith once delivered to the saints;" and, as she herself expresses it, "This is exceeding good news, and by this means I hope poor neglected Orkney will have a share of the best of all blessings enjoyed on this side of the rest prepared for the followers of the Lamb."

It was her privilege to see two places of worship belonging to the Baptists built on the island; and in the year 1844, she took a lively interest in the great increase the church received to its members, partly through the labours of their young pastor, Mr Henry Harcus At this time she also became anxious that a minister from the south would visit the dear church with which she was wont to associate. Accordingly, after repeated solicitations, Mr Johnston, then of Cupar, now of Edinburgh, visited the island in 1845, which gave her no small joy; and although she was prevented being at the house of prayer, yet she rejoiced at seeing others benefited and souls brought under the sound of the gospel; and it was a great source of enjoyment to her to listen to what her husband and friends could communicate of what they heard of the good word of life.

To her friends it appeared that she could not be much longer a sojourner in this vale of tears. Her disease, although particularly painful, she bore with uncommon patience, and in a letter to a friend, speaking of her confinement to bed, she says- "To be in bed a week is to some thought a prison, but to be confined four years and never able to rise or lie, looks like a prison indeed but it is the Lord's will, and oh that he may never suffer me to repine at his doings, for I know that it shall all be well." During the last nine weeks she was only able to be once lifted out of bed, and frequently did she ask dear friends by whom she was surrounded if they thought her end was nigh? If they answered no, she generally wept - her desire was to be absent from the body and present with the Lord. Shortly before she ceased to speak, she said to her husband, "Through the course of this illness, which has been long, I have had several trials of a spiritual nature, but now *the victory is won*". To each of her domestics she gave a dying injunction, but afterwards she spoke very little, her sufferings were so great; and on August 10th 1846, her heavenly Father saw meet to release her from pain by taking her to himself.

The Sabbath after her death, her funeral sermon was preached from these words, which she herself selected, "By grace are you saved."

Thus lived and died one, who, though in comparative private life was an ornament to her profession, and in whose history we may find this lesson, that however situated in life, we may find a means of manifesting that we are truly on the Lord's side.

Written by *Eliza Johnston*, in an article in *The Evangelist,* June 1847 found in Belltowers, Westray.

Other Historical Personalities

James Scott, Trenabie, Westray

James Scott, born in 1824 son of David Scott of Trenabie appears in the 1851 census as a Baptist Missionary although he had had ministerial training before that time. His field of mission was mainly the islands of Eday, Sanday and Burray as well as helping in Westray. He often worked alongside Henry Harcus who was his brother-in-law. His wife was Ellen Seatter and Henry was married to her sister Phyllis. His missionary tours to Burray during the years 1848 – 1850 produced much fruit as he baptised twenty-six people taking the church roll to sixty nine. He was only in his early twenties at the time.

He went on to have a remarkable ministry in Caithness. He was called to Keiss, the oldest Baptist Church in Scotland in 1865. There he continued an itinerant ministry. When he left in 1883 to go to Scarfskerry there were one hundred members at Keiss, twenty one at Stroma, twenty two at Freswick and many faithful supporters besides.

James Scott led a similar pastorate in Scarfskerry until he retired in 1902. It was said later that, "His name was still fragrant throughout the district and his work abides".

He and his wife ended their days at the Vestry in Westray at the site of the Tabernacle so it may still have been Baptist Church property. James died in 1904 and Ellen in 1905.

*Kenneth Scott, a kinsman and fellow missionary, reading from
James Scott's Bible at the desk he used in the Vestry*

James Balfour, Chalmersquoy, Westray

James Balfour was born at Chalmersquoy in 1858. His parents were
David Balfour and Barbara Reid. He went to Edinburgh University
and graduated with a Master of Arts degree. A quote from the book
"Revival in Rose Street", the history of Charlotte Baptist Chapel,

written by his kinsman, Dr Ian
Balfour says it was noted that,
"unlike many students he had
been regular in his attendance
at the services of the sanctuary,
and had ever been ready to co-
operate in various branches of
the Chapel's Christian work.
His interest in overseas mission
was awakened in childhood by
reading the *Juvenile Baptist
Herald*.

(David Balfour pictured left)

He went on to prepare himself for missionary work and was appointed tutor at the Calabar Missionary College in Kingston, Jamaica. He was ordained and valedicted from the Chapel in 1881. He settled in Jamaica and his son David became Registrar General in Jamaica.

Some of the family visited Westray in May 2008.

Capt. John Craigie, FSA Scot., 1865 – 1944

Capt. John Craigie was a deacon and secretary of the Westray Baptist Church for many years. He was born into a Christian home in Rousay but did not become a Christian himself until he was about forty years old. Until then he had acted like one in that he sang in the church choir, taught in the Sunday school and was a church member. It was the death of his fourteen year old daughter that finally touched his heart in 1902.

He was a popular master mariner and had been captain on several of the North Isles steam boats. He was the first master on the Earl Thorfinn when she came to Orkney in 1928. To mark his promotion to this new ship the islanders presented him with a gold watch and £44 as a mark of the esteem and regard that they felt for him. He had previously been captain on the Orcadia and the Fawn. The shipping company manager had once said, "Don't you be worried about the Fawn. As long as Craigie is in her he'll keep water under her".

He also took his responsibilities in the church seriously. He took the Bible Class, was Sunday School Superintendent and kept very full and well written minutes of the diaconate meetings. For some years in his retirement he took on to pastor the Baptist churches in Sanday and Eday coming back to be a deacon and elder in WBC in 1933.

Miss Barbara Balfour, Chalmersquoy, Westray

Barbara Balfour was born 1880 the youngest of David Balfour and Barbara Reid's family. There were eight boys and three girls. As a family they were very supportive to the Westray Baptist Church. Her oldest brother James was a Baptist Missionary and had gone to Jamaica but her brother Murdoch was a deacon, secretary and treasurer for many years in WBC. He died suddenly in October 1917 the day following a deacons meeting. He had made a generous donation to the WBC Centenary Fund in 1910 and his legacy of £500 became known as the Balfour Bequest and was invested for the benefit of the Church. Barbara would always remind us, "We are just stewards of what we have" so that seems to be a tenet the family lived by. Barbara was a schoolteacher but did not teach very long. She looked after the farm on her own with a reliable staff but did teach for a time in the Sunday School. At least once she trained some pupils to pass a test from the Scottish Baptist Union. (See page 8). She was well respected and was called on to help the deacons in different ways.

Chalmersquoy, taken around 1925 with staff outside the kitchen door

When she died in 1959 that made her the longest lived of the family and the last to bear the much respected name of Balfour in Westray.

James Rendall Thomson, Fueld, Westray

Rev James Rendall Thomson, born June 1902, was the son of David Thomson, a deacon in WBC, and his wife Jessie nee Rendall. He was one of a family of six. Jim was a haemophiliac so could not take part in the rough and tumble way of life that his playmates enjoyed. Nevertheless he had a lovely nature and was always full of fun. He read and studied his Bible, became a Christian early in life and showed a gift for preaching.

He applied to Spurgeon's College, London in 1921 for training which was ambitious for anyone in the post war years. WBC did not support him directly but the deacons formed a "Finance Committee" and raised the money by asking for donations.

Jim, or Jeemo o' Fueld as he was fondly called, had a very successful ministry at Millbrook Baptist Church, Southampton. Recently, because of parish boundary changes, the church changed its name to Freemantle Baptist Church.

One winter's night he left a group of carol singers to go home to prepare for a funeral the next day. He rode a motorcycle and on his way he was hit by another motorcyclist and died in a London Hospital soon after from his injuries in December 1962. He was well loved and respected for his many good works in Southampton. He was a part time Free Church Chaplain to the Southampton General Hospital and was highly thought of there. For many years he was missionary secretary and worked hard within the Boys' Brigade. In recognition of all that he did a Thomson Memorial Hall was built at the church in his memory and is used to the present day. His beloved wife Rosa laid the foundation stone.

Thomson Memorial Hall, Southampton.

THE THOMPSON MEMORIAL HALL.

This Hall was erected to the glory of God and in memory of the Rev. James Thompson. Pastor of this Church 1936-1962, through the generosity of Mrs Rose Thompson and the Members and Friends of the Millbrook Baptist Church.

"The memory of the righteous is a blessing".
Proverbs. 10·7.

Jim regularly came to Westray on holiday and was often asked to preach at more than one of the Westray Churches. His Westray accent got a good airing and he seemed to always choose hymns with a lot of "aights" in them! In the early days Rev John Lawrie had encouraged him and later in life he spent many happy times with Rev James Pottinger.

Jack Scott was brave enough to take the two of them to fish for cuithes on a summer's evening. It was well into the night before the cuithes were fried and eaten with bere bunnos and Orkney butter.

Jim Thomson was proud of Westray and Westray was proud of him.

Jim Thomson pictured with his wife, Rosa.

Jeemie Drever, Beuith, Westray

One of the greatest losses to the Westray Baptist Church in recent years was the passing of James Alexander Drever (Jeemie) after a relatively short illness, on 10th April 1999 at the age of 56 years. The funeral, a few days later, saw the biggest gathering of people in and around the church that had been seen in living memory and perhaps for decades before. He was very popular and had many friends in the farming world and also in the business world from the time when he had been a general merchant and butcher. The latter meant he worked long hours often just to oblige his customers. He was also a special constable with the Northern Constabulary.

Nearest his heart was the Lord's work in the chapel. He became a very young deacon in 1962. Although he was shy as a young boy he learned "to speak in public in the Christian Endeavour" as many others had done. He soon appeared to have a real gift for public speaking along with a great sense of humour. Over the years he did sterling work with the young folk of the church in Sunday School and Christian Endeavour. He could make things interesting for children with quizzes and competitions etc. He was also very talented musically.

He, along with George Rendall ran the CE camps all over Orkney and Caithness for many years. One day he had a reckoning on a jotter and realised that over half of the island's population had been with the CE to camp or had attended the weekly meetings. When the camps restarted after a break in 1998 Jeemie was there to instruct the new generation of leaders. With his energetic leadership (both day and night!) he proved a hard act to follow.

When he was at the Kirkwall Grammar School he had an accident and cut his hand quite badly when he fell against a phone kiosk. After it was stitched at the hospital he asked if he would be able to play the piano after this. He was assured he could and so he replied, "That's grand as I couldn't do it before". They were proved wrong so he had to look for a wife who could play a keyboard! His eye fell on Kathleen Rendall, Breckowall, and they made a great team. They both sang with the group known as the "Rays".

In 2005 Westray Baptist Church needed a new roof. It was decided to hold a "Tribute Concert" using the songs and music of the Rays and of the late Pat Jamieson a Baptist friend from Lerwick, as a fund raising effort. It was called the "The Raise the Roof Fund". The Old Kirk was packed for the occasion. Michael and Teenie sang with the remaining Rays and Pat's wife Lorna and his three sons sang Pat's songs. Then a united choir including Jeemie's great friends Ivan Rendall and Graham Maben, sang some of Pat's and the Rays' special songs. One came away with the feeling that both Jeemie and Pat had lived perhaps short but fulfilled lives in the service of their Lord. *(Jeemie pictured right rowing through the Scaun's arch.)*

Jack Scott, Skaill, Westray - written by Kay Gordon

Jack Scott was a very well known public figure throughout the islands, not only as a successful farmer, but also for his service to the community as a Council member. His talents and interests were many and wide-ranging, being a Captain on land, sea and air as well as a deputy lieutenant for Orkney.

He was, true to Westray tradition, an expert boatman. Francis Gordon, who was pastor for several years in Kirkwall Baptist Church, shared his love of the sea. 'Once,' he recalls, 'it was after midnight, and we were sailing Jack's boat, the *Coriander,* from Westray to Kirkwall. We had just had a drink of tea, and with a brief instruction to me to "just keep the Cathedral tower in line with the end of the Shapinsay land", he went below to wash the cups. That was no problem - until the floodlight on the Cathedral spire was switched off. There we were, heading blind on a flood tide for the gap between Shapinsay and the Vasa Skerry! I shouted down to him, and he called back, "What was your heading when the light went out?" I told him. "That's fine," he said calmly. "Just keep that heading, and we'll clear Vasa." And we did.'

His plane too became a familiar sight over Orkney. Francis flew with Jack a number of times between Kirkwall and Westray, and also to Eday and Sanday, but there was one occasion that is vividly etched in his memory. 'After giving me a very few minutes' instruction, he let me have the controls as we flew up the west side, round Noup Head and turned towards his landing field at Skaill. All the while he sat there as if he didn't have a nerve in his body, as this total novice flew his precious plane. Then came the question:
"D'you see the red and white board at the far side of the field?"
"Yes…"
"Then if you keep that halfway up the windscreen, you're coming in at a steady rate of descent"- pause – "mind you, if you pursue that too far, you'll hit the board, so perhaps I'd better do the landing!!"

Jack was a devoted family man, and he and Nan were famed for their generous hospitality. He loved to entertain visitors, building lasting friendships across the world.

But the chief love of his life was his Saviour. He served all his days as a member, then deacon, of Westray Baptist Church, and for no less than 43 years as its secretary, steering the way through several vacancies, and befriending and supporting each pastor called to the charge.

It was a joy and a pleasure to welcome him into our congregation when he retired to Kirkwall, and one particularly poignant memory is of a night when he gave his testimony, and sang that lovely old Gospel song:
*"By and by, when I look on His face,
Beautiful face, thorn shadowed face;
By and by when I look on his face,
I'll wish I had given Him more…"*

Jack pictured left, enjoying retirement

27

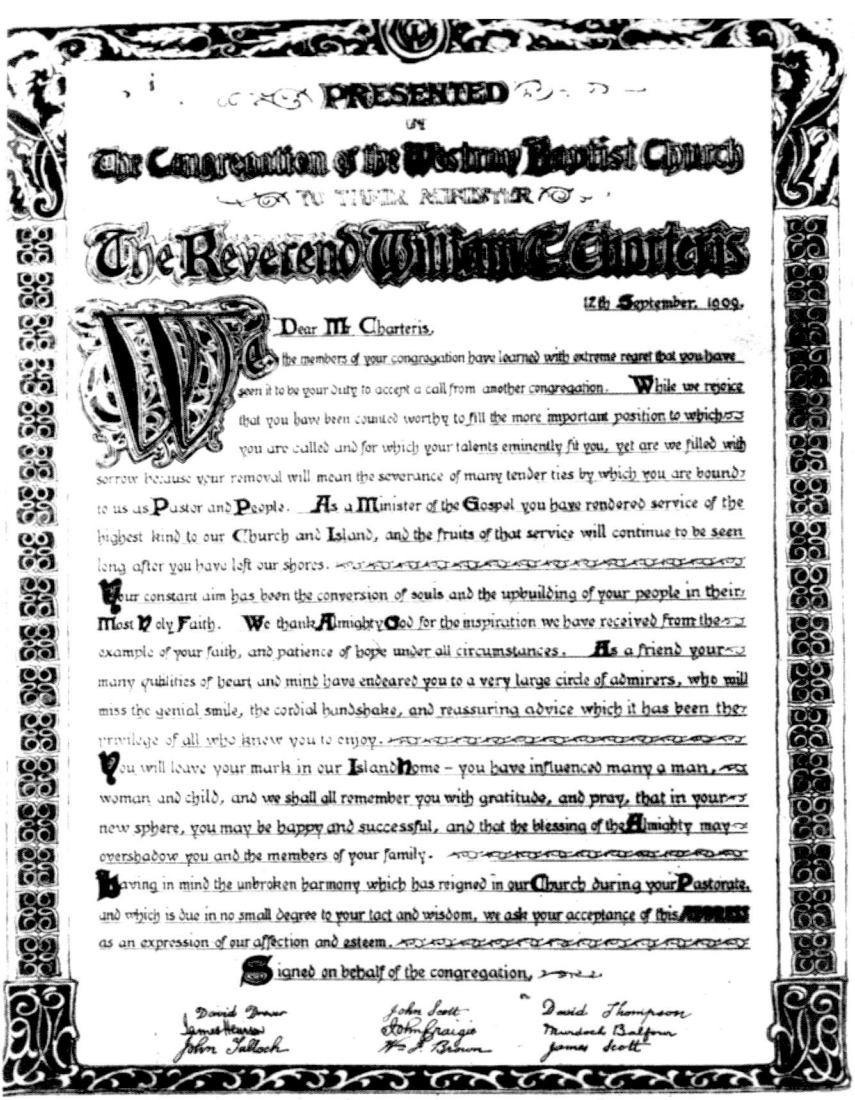

A certificate presented to Rev. Charteris in 1909 showing how highly the Westray Baptist Kirk thought of their minister.

Memories of Ministers

1. William Tulloch 1810-1858, came from North Ronaldsay and was working as a cabinet maker in Kirkwall when James Haldane was on his preaching tour of Orkney. James was so impressed with

his Christian witness that he made it possible financially for William to get training in the south and then to return and evangelise the North Islands of Orkney. He chose Westray as his base initially and was later to become the first Baptist minister in the Westray Church although not the first one of the group to accept baptism! He laboured long and diligently for many years and a visitor recorded hearing him leading in prayer at a service when he was ninety years old.

2. Henry Harcus 1843 – 1868 was born at Swartmill, Westray, into a Christian family. It was also a family that was renowned, even to

the present day, for its men who were such good boat builders. They built traditional Westray skiffs. After his schooling at the island school he worked at home and did some fishing, buying a share in a herring boat. He was converted, baptised and joined the Baptist church in 1827. He moved to Kirkwall with his young wife in 1838 to study under the Rev T Macken, pastor of the Independent Church there.

After two winters study he returned to Westray and moved into the Baptist Manse so that he could help William Tulloch who had already served as minister for forty years. Some time later he was able to do a time of study at a college in Cupar. He had a successful ministry with many people joining the church and during revival times 57 people were baptised and added to membership in the year 1860. He had been labouring in Westray as well as helping in Sanday, Eday and Burray for nearly thirty years when nearly two thirds of the Westray membership went over to the Christian Brethren. This broke his heart. He felt he could not go on. Many tried to encourage him to stay, including the Rev Dr Oliver Flett who travelled especially to Westray to do that but he moved on to Canada in 1869 and preached there for ten years. On his return to this country Burray Baptist church called him in 1879. This church enjoyed seven years of peace and harmony under his ministry and quite a number were baptised before he had to retire "because of infirmities of old age". He spent his last years with family in Ayr, where he died in 1899. He had been a faithful worker for his Lord and his fellow man. His legacy, his book on, "The History of the Orkney Baptist Churches" has been an inspiration and a source of information for many over the years.

3. Rev George MacDonald 1870-1875 was sent to the Westray Baptist Church by the Home Mission to help after Henry Harcus left for Canada. Gavin Mowat came from Shetland to assist at that time. It is interesting to note that there were no more local Orcadian leaders in the church until the induction of James Miller in 1984.

4. J A Marnie 1879 – 1881 came to Orkney straight from training college and had been minister in Eday for three years before coming to Westray to preach for a further three years. A daughter Maggie Alice was born at the manse in 1878. He went on to settle in John Street, Coatbridge, before emigrating to Canada.

5. P F Slater 1881– 1894 We know that he was born in Canada but the family were staying in Dennistoun, Glasgow when he came to Westray. His records of membership are the earliest that we have. They read as if society was going through a bad patch during his ministry. Times were hard, population was at its highest so there was less to go around and many young folk succumbed to tuberculosis. The staff of life, home brewed ale, led to the downfall of some. Members were being "rebuked, admonished and remonstrated with" regarding their immoral conduct, all to no effect sometimes. Some did acknowledge their faults, profess repentance and would then be retained as members.

Family history shows that in 1889 Peter Forrester Slater then aged 33 years got married to Mary Rosie from Gill Pier. Her father was an engineer. They went on to have two daughters born in the manse, Mary in 1890 and Jessie in 1892. He was remembered as being the first person to own a bicycle in Westray. He was presented with a purse of sovereigns by the church in order to buy a gold watch. After leaving Westray they moved to Riding Mill, Newcastle on Tyne, now part of Stocksfield Baptist Church.

6. Rev John Yeomans 1895 – 1900 appears to have been educated in Manchester. He preached in Eday and Westray over the years 1894 – 1900. He also served as president of the Young People's Christian Endeavour Society (YPSCE) in 1897. He received a unanimous call to Lossiemouth Baptist Church and was in that pastorate for fourteen years. Following this he went south to Middleton Junction Church in Manchester.

7. Rev Albert Griffiths. 1901 – 1905. Mr Griffiths came to Westray from Birmingham. At his induction he was highly recommended by speakers from the south. One of the deacons certainly approved of him and called his son Albert Griffiths Brown as a tribute to the minister. A year later Albert and Ellen (nee Burton) had their own child, Albert Edward Griffiths in 1902 and in 1904 William Henry Griffiths was born. Mr Griffiths was in Burray 1905 – 1909 and later moved to

Edinburgh 1909 – 1923,where he had a successful ministry in Abbeyhill Baptist Church.

8. Rev William Cramb Charteris 1905 – 1909. Westray Baptist Church witness was very positive during the ministry of Mr Charteris. Improvements to the buildings were planned and carried out. The new hall gave space for a Bible Class, lantern lectures were introduced for youth work, music became part of the services and district meetings became regular features etc. There was a dramatic increase in membership following special missions.

He was a newly married man when he came to Westray with his young wife Jane. Their daughter Ena was born in the manse. When they left Westray they went to the Baptist Church in Ayr. He spent the war years as a chaplain in the army receiving an OBE and an MC. He finished a successful ministry in Ayr before he went on to witness in Stirling Baptist Church.

9. Rev William Gilmour 1909 – 1916 came to Westray from The Gordon Mission in Aberdeen. Following the BU exam he was accepted as a Baptist minister and Westray was his first charge. He encouraged evangelistic missions and had some of his friends from the Gordon Mission conduct them. Both he and Mrs Gilmour were noted for their hospitality in the manse and for providing teas at public meetings. It fell to him to organise the centenary celebrations in 1910. He chaired the meetings, welcoming many dignitaries from near and far. He had a lovely singing voice and at one of these meetings he sang with Mrs and Miss Brown.

From Westray he was called to Fraserburgh in 1916. He pastored several churches across Scotland in later years and was still in charge at Hopeman, Morayshire in 1953.

10. Rev Edward McGough Hogg 1917-1927 came to Westray in 1917. He was an Englishman and had already served two years in Burray. He actually came on the recommendation of a former Westray minister in the person of Albert Griffiths. The church provided him with a motorbike for transport in Westray but he had to rely on boats to take him to the other islands and to Shetland where he missioned on occasions.

He had married Mary Anne Carter the year he came to Westray. A daughter Evelyn was born in 1918 and a son Aubrey in 1921. However before this one of the deacons, Tom Bain had a son in 1917 whom he named Edward McGough Hogg Bain. Thankfully he became known as Mac Bain! Being musical both Tom and Mr Hogg would have had a lot in common. In 1926 Edward Hogg got a call to Bayswater Church in Western Australia. Conditions here were inferior in every way to what he had left in Westray with no motor bike in all his time there! However, he felt it was God's call and he spent twenty six years in that church.

In addition he helped found the Perth Bible Institute. He served as chairman, lecturer, public advocate and preacher until his death in 1953. A fellow minister summed up his life when he said "The Rev Hogg was a good fellow, a good preacher and a good Baptist with a not-always-obvious sense of humour! A personal tragedy was the loss of his son Aubrey, a fine singer and organist. He was killed on active service with the RAAF when the Lancaster bomber on which he was an air gunner crashed in Yorkshire. His sister Evelyn, along with her daughter Marilyn Seton, visited Orkney a few years ago and met Mac Bain her father's god son.

11. Rev John Lawrie 1927 – 1942 was appointed minister of the Westray Baptist Church by the Baptist Home Mission of Scotland. He commenced his pastorate of fifteen years on the 4th September

1927. The first marriage that he officiated at was when he married Thomas Mowat Pottinger, Knugdale and Betsy Cooper, Easthill on 15th September. (Parents of the author!)

Mr Lawrie was a faithful preacher of the gospel with a special love and concern for the young. Very soon after he arrived John Robert Mowat and George Gray Thomson were baptised and welcomed into Membership. They along with John Scott Drever had been meeting together for bible study and when Mr Lawrie picked up on this he organised a very successful Christian Endeavour group that continued in Westray for nearly eighty years.

Mr Lawrie was a faithful visitor, and often with his wife Janet, would visit homes at quite a distance away. The local taxi, Jeemsie o' Saverton would drop them at the most distant point in their itinerary and fetch them again at an arranged place in the evening. His visits were usually jolly and Mrs Lawrie enjoyed a laugh but he never left the home without reading the bible and making a prayer as well as leaving a tract.

In those days the minister and his wife were never called by their first name or just a second name but Mr Lawrie got a surprise one day when he was crossing a fence with Jim Thomson and Jim ripped his coat on the fence. Jim let out a roar, "Oh, Lorry me cot".

Mr and Mrs Lawrie retired to Castlebrae in 1942 and Mrs Lawrie died in 1944 aged 64 and was buried in Westray. Mr Lawrie moved to Stow in the Borders where he remarried. He was buried in Edinburgh.

12.   Rev James Pottinger 1947-1959 was a Shetland man and his wife Helen was also from Shetland.   He came to the Westray Baptist Church in 1942.   He had been the minister for the Eday and Sanday Baptist Churches since 1936.   Prior to that he had begun his ministry in 1925 as Pastor of the

Lunnasting and Sandsting Baptist Churches in Shetland. He was said to labour with great zeal in both districts and gave himself unstintingly for eleven years.

While he was busy there he was also busy corresponding with Helen Burgess who was a nurse and working with the South African General Mission in Africa. She returned to Shetland and they married before coming to Orkney.

Westray found them both to be deeply spiritual people. They were good preachers and Helen could step in and conduct a service whenever she was needed. She was also called on to help with nursing duties from time to time. James too had a pair of good hands and willingly helped the whosoever as a joiner or a watch maker etc. He was the Baptist minister but it was said that the whole island was his parish. There were many stories of their generosity with their time and their substance. Helen was known on at least one occasion to part with the coat off her own back!

Helen and James Pottinger

The life of the church thrived during the sixteen years of this ministry. It had begun when there was a war on and evangelistic meetings and missions became common. Notable were the Faith Mission meetings that went on for six nights of the week for about a month at a time. There were more prayer meetings in the church and the manse and there were new and more modern ways introduced in the work among the young folk. Mrs Pottinger as she was always called in Westray would have groups of girls in the manse to learn how to bath and handle babies, how to bake or sew and at the same time teaching them Christian things from the Bible. Mr Pottinger too would have boys in the garage working with wood.

The manse shed needed to get a bigger door when the Pottingers arrived as they were the first tenants to own a car. It was an open top model that had come from Shetland with them. It was fondly known as the Hallelujah Chariot and lots of folk enjoyed a ride in it. Hallelujah was a favourite word of Mr Pottinger's as he did believe in "Praising the Lord" at all times. When he intimated the hymns during a service he would add the words, "Pit in the pairts" eyeing the young men in the choir especially. He encouraged group singing to the extent that he was asked to bring artistes with him when he went preaching at other places.

Both the Pottingers were greatly missed when they retired back to Shetland in 1959. Mr Pottinger died in 1961 but Mrs Pottinger was spared to do some more nursing notably in Fair Isle. She made some return visits to Westray as well where she and her husband had given so much of themselves. Mr Pottinger had always had a dream to see a Baptist Church in Kirkwall. He lived to see that dream fulfilled when twenty five people from the Westray Baptist Church settled in Kirkwall around 1954. A church was founded there in1959. At the present time it continues to grow and is a living testimony of the faithful teaching and witness of James and Helen Pottinger.

13. Rev Kenneth Denman 1959 -1960 acted as Westray Baptist Church pastor for a year after the Pottingers retired although he was still a student at the time. He stayed in the manse on his own but with some mothering from the deacons' wives he got on very well. He took a very active part in all aspects of the church work especially the Sunday School and Christian Endeavour. He left in 1960 to complete a college course and then returned to Orkney as minister of Kirkwall Baptist Church.

14. Rev James Alexander Brydon Maben 1960 – 1963 written by his son Graham Maben.

My Dad, Brydon Maben, who passed away in May 1995, was Westray Baptist Kirk Minister, from September 1960 until September 1963. I was 11 years old at that time and remember very clearly the move my family made to Westray. At that time, there was Mum and Dad, my older sister Dorothy and my younger sister Barbara. Karen came along 6 months later. Oh, and there was Peter the cat!

The trip involved boarding the St. Ninian at Leith and sailing via Aberdeen to Kirkwall – that was an adventure in itself, but the best was yet to come. The trip to Westray was aboard the old Earl Thorfinn. Our possessions were in a trailer unit which accompanied us the whole way.

On Wednesday 21st September, when we arrived at Gill Pier, Westray, there was an army of Kirk folk there to meet us. My memory tells me that the steamer arrived around 2 p.m. We were whisked away to Skaill by Jack Scott. There we were introduced to his wife, Nan, her daughters, Linda, Margaret and Fiona and Auntie Johan and Nan's Dad, Tom.

The table groaned under the sheer weight of the food upon it! This, we learned very quickly, was the norm in every household we visited!

Linda took Dorothy and me around the farm and down to the shore overlooking the Holm of Aikerness. The day was a beautiful, flat calm sunny day and I remember thinking I must have died and gone to heaven! What a place and what lovely people.

My Dad had, as early as I can recall, been an active member of Victoria Street Baptist Kirk in Galashiels, where we lived. He was a deacon and regularly took services at the kirk and also the sister kirk in Stirling Street. He was an electrician and, just before moving to Westray, had taken a position as Manager of an electrical retailer in Galashiels. Incidentally, they fired him, when he told them, casually one day, he was studying to become a minister!

He was passionate about music – in particular, Brass Band and Male Voice. He had been a Member of the Border Male Voice Quartet since it was founded in the early 1950's and had toured and recorded with them. He also played solo trombone in Galashiels Brass Band.

Mum and Dad were delighted to have been called by the Westray Baptist Kirk. Mum set about getting to know people and founded the Women's Auxiliary, whilst Dad got down to the serious business of his ministry.

His love of Male Voice led him to form the Westray Male Voice Choir. I can remember him coming back from the evening service and telling Mum about all the terrific singers he could hear from the pulpit. His ear was very good and he could pick out one person and tune in. He decided to make an open invitation to the Westray Kirks for any men who wished to be involved in a Male Voice Choir, to come along to the Baptist Kirk after the evening service.

The result was amazing. After several months of practice and perfecting, the Choir went on tour. It later made several records and was a great success long after Dad left Westray, due to the dedication and hard work of those involved.

In 1963, my family left - leaving me behind to finish school. I stayed on a further 2 years, working as a farmhand at Skaill, before leaving to take up work down south. I loved Westray so much, my wife and I returned and settled in 2004!

Mum and Dad would love to have been here to join in the 200th Anniversary celebrations, so on their behalf, can I congratulate Westray Baptist Kirk on achieving this.

15. Rev Harry Telfer 1963 – 1970 writes as follows:

It all started with a letter from Jack Scott inviting Brenda and I to spend two Sundays in the Westray Church back in September 1963.

We had recently married in Worthing, Sussex following my training at London Bible College. Brenda was a teacher in London. Although I had been accepted for Ministry by the Scottish Baptist Union we had to go to the map to find out where Westray was.

We well remember the day when we stepped off the Orcadia on to Gill Pier for the first time. Jack Scott was there to meet us, and the warmth of his welcome together with the warmth of the sun made us feel from that first moment that this was the place of God's appointing for our first ministry.

We were soon introduced to a warm hearted Gospel loving people, and to a Church with an intriguing history. Born out of James Haldane's tour of the Orkney Islands in 1797, the new fellowship met with stern opposition and was refused accommodation for their worship services. At last room was found in the great dark Banqueting Hall of Noltland Castle. Baptisms were performed in nearby Burness Loch, and so the Baptist Church was formed in the summer of 1810. In time the shrub planted that day, grew into a tree of considerable size. Back in 1963 the island had a much larger population than it has today. There were three active Churches together with a Brethren Assembly. These three Churches worked together in such a way that we enjoyed an unusual sense of unity. We left Westray in 1970 to take up the charge at Alloa Baptist Church. Yet such is the love that we have for the island, the people and the Church, that we have gone back for holidays most years. In some sense when we drive up from Fife to Scrabster we feel that we are going home! There are so many memories of the seven years that we spent in Westray Baptist Church. Let us share with you just a few of them.

Memories of our two daughters Linda and Rosemary who were born in the Manse. We later learned that Linda was the first girl to be born in the Manse since Evelyn Hogg some 45 years before. Both girls continue to speak proudly of their Westray roots.

Memories of the Youth Fellowship that met in the Chip Shop at Claybraes. What a privilege it was to meet with young folk from three of the island churches on a Sunday evening at 8pm. It was in these days that the "Chippie Band" was formed.

Memories of a trip to Shetland with the Bible Class and Friends. Thanks to the support given by Orkney County Council, we were able to fly the Bible Class together with some of their school friends to Dunrossness in Shetland. We went there at the invitation of the Pastor of the Baptist Church, Robert Hughes. Zena Bain (Hutchison) was our cook, and for many of us it proved to be a very special time. It was a time when many of these young folk met with the Lord in a new way.

Memories of the Male Voice Choir and their inter island visits. We know so many Orcadians who have never had the privilege of visiting all of the North Isles. For the Male Voice Choir, their summer programme included visits to a number of the North Isles year by year in company with the Kirkwall section. It was always such a thrill to gather with the local folk in an evening of praise. "What a day it will be" and "When the roll is called up yonder I'll be there!"

Memories of the Christian Endeavour Camp in Hoy 1968. Brenda will never forget her trip across the Westray Firth on her way to camp It was one of these days when all of the kids were sick. Not a good beginning for camp. Fortunately the weather improved and the camp went well. Brenda and Irene Miller (Stout) were the cooks and the folk from Howe in Stromness sent over milk each day by boat. Ward Hill, the Dwarfie Stone and the Longhope Lifeboat were all on the itinerary. It was a sad day in 2007 when we returned to Westray to attend the closing rally for CE on the island.

Like the writer to the Hebrews in the New Testament, we would have to say in all sincerity, "Time would fail me to tell...". We do thank God every day for the love, support and kindness of the Fellowship in Westray Baptist Church.

16. Rev Raymond Thompson 1971 – 1977 writes as follows:

I served the Westray Baptist Church for 6 years from 1971-1977. It was my first Pastorate and I gained valuable experience for future ministry. I loved the island and its people. Margaret and I have many happy memories of our time on the Island.

When I first set foot on Westray I was a bachelor boy but when I left I had increased in goods having gained a wife, a daughter, a cat and a Shetland collie dog!

There were many humorous situations I encountered over the years. At one point we had a visit from the then secretary of the Scottish Baptist Union, Andrew MacRae. One evening I was playing table tennis with him out at Skaill and seemed to be winning. Out of the blue there came a shout from the youngest of the Scott family "Come on Tomo." These words sounded familiar as I was sometimes called by that name during my college days.

On another occasion after a morning service little Jack Bain from Broughton (who will be a big Jack now) said to me "You prayed for yourself this morning" I said, "What do you mean Jack?" He said. "You gave thanks for food and Raymond." Then I remembered that during the first prayer I had been thanking God for food and raiment!

During my spell in Westray I helped out for a short spell driving Bain's grocery van and one day Annie Harcus and I got stuck as we were heading towards the Pier. All of a sudden the van conked out and Annie and I were left stranded at the side of the road. We got in touch with Alistair and he came along in another vehicle to give us a pull. The rope broke but Alistair didn't know and went off on his own for quite some distance before realising what had happened and left us once again, stranded. It caused a bit of a laugh to some people who saw all this and also to those who heard about it.

Margaret, my wife, recalls the night when the lights went out in the church during an evening service and we were all left in darkness. Two deacons sprinted down to the manse to see what had happened and found that Margaret had overloaded the power system by putting on a heater!

It was good to be with you for those six years as your pastor and it was so encouraging to see people coming to a saving knowledge of Christ. Amidst all the laughter and various incidents this is the most important thing of all.

17. Rev Foster Wright 1977 – 1983 writes as follows:

My first contact with Westray was in 1975, while in Kirkwall on holiday from Ireland. I must confess until I went to Kirkwall Baptist Church, on our first Sunday in the 'Toon', I had never even heard of Westray. However it turned out that Kirkwall Baptist Church in those days was comprised mainly of Westray exiles. I heard so much about this wonderful Isle to the North that as a family we decided to pay a visit before our holiday came to a close. The visit was in fact a camping trip, on our arrival, we found what we thought was an ideal site, right on the beach with the sound of Atlantic breakers in our ears.

However in a very short while, we were visited by a herd of very inquisitive cows. We were obviously on farm land and being good campers, we decided to ask permission from the owner of the land. The only farm we could see went by the name of Noltland, so up we went to ask permission. To our surprise we discovered that the farmers wife, not only knew we were camping on their land, she also knew who we were!! Ruby then invited us to join with them for a meal, at which we discovered that her husband Billy was a deacon at the Baptist church. After two days we returned to Kirkwall, never expecting to see Westray again, but we were wrong.

In 1977, through a mutual friend, we got an invite from the UF minister, the Rev Joe Creelman to holiday in Westray, the arrangement was that we would stay in the UF manse, and preach in the UF church on Sunday mornings and the Baptist church on Sunday evenings. Over the month we were there, we were asked if we would consider coming to live in Westray, as the Baptist church was vacant and looking for a minister. As it happened I was thinking of moving from the church I pastored in Belfast. However everything was put on hold as the church secretary, Jack Scott, was away South at the wedding of one of his daughters. Jack returned on our last Sunday, and an informal approach was made to me to see if I would be interested in being the pastor of Westray Baptist Church. I was delighted at the prospect and a formal call soon followed. As a family we moved to Westray at the end of October 1977. As a family, looking back on our years in Westray, we count them some of the happiest years of our lives.

During our time in Westray a number of changes took place, in regards to the church building and Westray life as a whole. Shortly after we arrived the new kitchen and toilets were completed, and then a few years later the Hydro arrived.

For me one of the highlights of my time there was the opportunities I got to take the gospel to other Islands. Sanday had a church building but no members and I was able to visit it with mission teams, and over the summer as the result of the gift of an old caravan and car, to have services two or three times a month. Stronsay was a place where there were church members but no building, I managed to visit there a number of times and have services in the home of Jimmy and Ivy Stout.

Then there was Egilsay, one of the inner Isles that I visited a number of times with the Rev Francis Gordon from Kirkwall. However these visits would have been well nigh impossible without the help of Jack Scott, who often provided me with an air service in his little plane. I always found it a bit ironic that the call sign of the plane was 'Whiskey Hotel' - maybe not the most appropriate call sign for the secretary of the Baptist Kirk. Jack's boat the "Coriander" was also used on many occasions skippered by Jack or Jimmy Drever. My full time ministry is now finished, but we will always be thankful to God for our wonderful years in Westray.

18. Rev Jim Miller 1983 – 1989 writes as follows:

After I had completed my studies at the Bible Training Institute and Scottish Baptist College from 1979-83, Jack Scott, secretary of the Westray Baptist Church, asked if I would take on a month of pulpit supply. We went as a family in August 1983, and on our return to Glasgow, the church called me to be their pastor. I accepted the call as I felt this was of God.

My Ordination took place in the Kirkwall Baptist Church in October 1983, followed by my Induction to the Westray Baptist Church a few days later. We were surrounded by family and friends from near and far, for this special time. Westray was no strange place for us to settle in and make our home as we were both born and brought up in Orkney. As a family, we had been on holiday in Westray in previous years and had relatives on the island. Irene's auntie Ruby was so pleased that we were coming to stay. Christine and James settled in well, and Christine still has contact with some of her friends.

Westray was a lovely place to begin my ministry. People were very kind and understanding. There were many opportunities to share the gospel in their homes and be involved with other churches. I was also welcomed into the school to take assemblies. People were very faithful in Sunday worship and in the midweek prayer meeting, and this encouraged me greatly. It was a great joy to me to have baptised 18 adults, including 5 members of family from the island of Stronsay. The weekly CE meetings were well attended under faithful leadership. The annual camps were always a highlight for both the young and not so young! It was at these camps that many young people made a commitment for the Lord. The Sunday School, Bible Class and the Pioneers were also led by committed leaders, and this encouraged the youngsters to come along. The Women's Auxiliary meetings were an encouragement for the ladies of the church, and they were able to share with other guilds on the island. It was a special occasion when they had an annual visit from the Scottish National WA President.

I had the pleasure of going with the Male Voice Choir as they went on tour in 1984, visiting many venues in Scotland. During our time in Westray, the church was privileged to have had many visits from guest speakers, missionaries and musicians.

There were "specials" for living on the island – e.g. a flight in Jack Scott's plane, or a sail in the 'Coriander', the boat that he built. He used both of them so willingly for the Lord's work.

My claim to fame is that I was descended from a young lad aged 6 years old, who was rescued from a Russian ship that was wrecked on Westray in the 1730s. He was the sole survivor and as the ship had come from Archangel, the boy was named Archie Angel. John Mason, my cousin and conductor of the Scottish Fiddle Orchestra, is 8th in direct line from Archie Angel.

19. Rev Archie McColl 1990- 1995 came to Westray in1990 from Cumbernauld Baptist Church where he had been for 23 years. He was a godly man, brought a depth of experience and quickly endeared himself to the congregation and the wider community. Archie is remembered for his strong, encouraging bible teaching, gentleness and dry sense of humour. In particular, friends in Westray remember his frequent references to Romans chapter 8 and the fact that with God on our side "we are more than conquerors through Him who loved us".

He was ably supported in his ministry by his wife Jean. She had been the National President of Women's Auxiliary in 1988 and was well known for her ministry in song at the meetings.

Even though his health was failing, Archie stayed on for a short time after retirement age to support the church. In 1995 he and Jean left to stay in Pittenweem not far from where his ministry started in Anstruther.

20. Rev Hugh McConnachie 1996 - 2001 writes about his time in Westray:

There was an immediate joy in my spirit on my first ever visit to Westray when I saw the extent of inter church fellowship. This deepened and brought assurance of my call to the ministry there.

Scotland and Orkney, including Westray was in the midst of a heavy snow fall when we arrived on the island, this prevented the Rev Ian Mundie flying from Glasgow for the Induction, so I preached my first sermon as Minister on the Sunday morning and was formally inducted to the charge by Rev Francis Gordon in the evening when he managed to get a ferry from Kirkwall. Thus began one of the most interesting and spiritually beneficial times in my life.

What immediately comes to mind when my heart *and* feet turn north is the warmth of the Westray folks and the great fellowship among the believers on the island.

During my ministry I had very supportive, dependable and spiritual men of God on the Diaconate. It certainly was not a 'one man band' as we were members of a leadership team that had a care for and over the church and island community.

I personally benefited from my fellowship with the other church leaders and it is a joy on my return visits to see joint church fellowship is still a priority on the island.

On our visit last year (2009) it was lovely to be part of a joint service in Kalisgarth care centre led by Mr Danny Harcus, that is true involvement, giving the older people an opportunity to worship with the church community.

Coming from a town background it was a revelation for me to be part of a farming community, meeting with farmers in byres and barns (I kept my 'wellies' in the boot of my car) and seeing the level of energy and commitment involved in the day to day joys and problems of working with animals and machinery.

The focus on youth in the Baptist Kirk was a priority, and the CE was still a regular weekly event. Our big daft cat Buz took delight in sneaking in to be with the young ones when no one was looking!

It was during our time in Westray that Michael and Christine Harcus and friends began to make CDs of their music ministry available for all to enjoy and receive blessing from. Fiona was privileged to have Michael, Christine and Mairi's music ministry at her inauguration in October 2009 as National President of the Scottish Baptist Women's Fellowship in its Centenary year. Fiona discovered a talent for puppetry through the encouragement of Rev Angus and his wife Dr Carol MacNeill, Westray's BMS link missionaries; she also enjoyed a weekly visit to the school with other ladies to help the children with knitting.

I had the joys of baptisms and weddings but also the sadness of burials, among these was the death of Mr Jimmy Drever which was so hard for his family, and a great loss to the Baptist Kirk and the whole island community.

It was also my privilege to minister to Davie and Maggie Burgher toward the end of their 75 years of marriage. Seeing Davy working on an Orkney chair, and also praying with Maggie after she had had her cataracts operated on, knowing that she could actually see me, was special.

I also have some comical moments to remember such as the day I visited a farm and was sitting speaking with the wife when her husband appeared in the kitchen doorway plus a strong smell of cow dung. He slowly revolved to reveal his back covered in cow manure. He had fallen backwards on the byre floor!

God granted Fiona and me a very special blessing in my call to the Baptist Kirk in Westray. We have too many memories for this short report, but the fact that we and our family can't keep away from the island shows our love for our church family there. We thank God for your love and continuing ministry to us both.

21   Rev Stephen Langford 2002 -2006 writes his reflections on God's calling to Westray,

Shall I abandon, O King of Mysteries, the soft comforts of home?
Shall I turn my back on my native land, and my face towards the sea?
Shall I put myself wholly at the mercy of God,
without silver, without horse, without fame and honour?
Shall I throw myself wholly on the King of kings,
without sword and shield, without food and drink, without a bed to lie on?
Shall I say farewell to my beautiful land, placing myself under Christ's yoke?
Shall I pour out my heart to him, confessing my
manifold sins and begging forgiveness, tears streaming down my cheeks?
Shall I leave the prints of my knees on the sandy beach,
a record of my final prayer in my native land?
Shall I then suffer every kind of wound the sea can inflict?
Shall I take my tiny coracle across the wide, sparkling ocean?
O King of Glorious Heaven, shall I go of my own choice upon the sea?
O Christ will you help me on the wild waves?

I first came across this prayer, known as Brendon's prayer on the mountain, in David Adam's book *A Desert in the Ocean*. As a result of my time in Westray this prayer, along with Psalm 137, became very precious to me and helped shape my ministry. Likewise, they have also been immensely helpful in reflecting back over my experience of Westray Baptist Church. Both the prayer and the Psalm have helped me place my experience of Westray into the wider context of God's grace and mercy.

It would be true to say that, as with the Israelites' time in Babylon, my time in Westray was not an easy one. However, just as the Israelites' exile produced some of the most creative and inspiring literature in the Bible, my time in Westray has proven to be a vital foundation for the ministry that God has continued to lead me into. As an island Westray held me fast when I would preferred to have followed Jonah's example and run away from the Lord's calling. Likewise, I learnt from many of Westray's folk that there are rich treasures waiting to be discovered by the person willing to practise a patient ministry built on the basics of prayer, preaching and pastoral visiting. In a sense the Baptist church in Westray became a finishing school where the Lord took the student fresh from college and shaped him into the pastor who would find an unexpected joy in further ministries. Because of this I am thankful and can, by God's grace, count my four years at Westray Baptist Church as an important time in the service of the Lord.

22   Rev Gavin Hunter   is the present minister of Westray Baptist Church.   Again we have a young pastor in his first church.   He comes from Edinburgh and has been pastoral assistant at Wester Hailes Baptist Church.   He has been aware of God's calling to the Baptist ministry since the age of seventeen. He did a Youth with a Mission discipleship course in Vancouver after leaving school he then went on to do a BD (hons) course in Theology and Pastoral Studies which he completed at the Scottish Baptist College.   He also had two placements one at Mosspark Baptist Church and the other at Granton Baptist Church.

We now look forward to what the Lord will do in this new ministry in the third century of the Westray Baptist Church's history.

Author visiting the grave of Henry Harcus, minister of Westray Baptist Church.
1843- 1868

Music & Singing in the Kirk

In the nineteenth century there was no instrumental music in the church. A person recognised to be a good singer was usually depended on to raise the tune for the psalm or hymn. One such was a deacon, William Pottinger of Knugdale. If he failed to hit the note at the first attempt then his wife Jean, nee Mowat, from Shetland stepped in immediately.

Rev William C Charteris became minister in November 1905. It is recorded that in December 1905 at a church meeting Murdoch Balfour submitted a unanimous resolution from the diaconate – purposing, "That the time had come when instrumental music might be introduced to aid the praise". Mr George Carter seconded and the resolution was cordially accepted, there being no dissenting voice. By January 1906 the gift of an organ from Mr W F Brown of Breckowall was accepted by the church.

The first organist was Mrs Jean Charteris, the minister's wife. Later a choir gathered near the organ at the front of the church. The organist then faced the pulpit where he or she could interpret the wishes of the preacher, and the precentor or choir leader stood beside it. The choir sat with their backs to the congregation and rose to face the body of the church during the singing.

Mr John Drever was a precentor when his son John Scott Drever became the organist at eleven years old in 1924. His teacher had been another minister Rev Edward Hogg. It must have pleased Mr Brown, the organ donor, when he saw how his family were able to take advantage of the musical opportunities on offer. His son Billy was a faithful and dependable precentor for many years. He was quiet, was never known to raise his voice but when he spoke you listened. He always encouraged his choir and then surprised them when he trained them to sing the Hallelujah Chorus from Handel's Messiah. It was so well received that it was sung to the public on two occasions.

Choir in 1950 Back row: Jack Scott, Mr Pottinger, George Rendall, John Harcus, Jimic Scott, Gavin Seatter, Billy Brown, Tommy Harcus,Jackie Mowat, Jim Brown. Front row: Mary Brown, Mrs Pottinger, Chrisabel Rendall, Rena Seatter, Nan Pottinger, Jeanie Cooper,Ruby Eunson, Helen Brown, Kitty Brown, Molly Rendall, Tanno Drever & John Drever.

Billy's younger brother Jim became precentor when he retired. Jim became famous as a soloist as well as a choir leader. On the distaff side of the family his daughter Helen had a strong and pleasant alto voice and she was also the church organist non-stop for 37 years. Then Jim's son Billy became known far and wide as a soloist as well as a member of the "Men of Orkney Choir", latterly as leader and conductor, and as one of a group known as "The Rays". His songs were often requested on radio programmes.

John Harcus, Jeemie & Kathleen Drever, Billy Brown, Isabell Harcus & Ivan Rendall

Both these groups made recordings that sold quite well. However they were not the first in this field. A church deacon, Thomas Pottinger Bain, born 1883 into the shop keeping and weaving family, also sang in the choir and then went on to sing solo. He was encouraged to go to Kirkwall and get Robbie Milne to make a 78 rpm record (or perhaps more than one). This was something new as a means of witnessing. One of his favourite hymns was

> "Singing I go along life's road,
> Praising the Lord, praising the Lord
> Singing I go along life's road
> For Jesus has lifted my load".

Back: Lois Buckley, Linda Scott Jack Scott Louise Drever and Tom Bain Front: Elizabeth Buckley, Margaret Scott & Fiona Scott, after church.

It was the custom for many years in the Westray Baptist Church for the morning service to be more of an exhortation to the Christians and the singing was from "Psalms and Hymns". That was followed with communion primarily for church members. However, the evening service attracted a greater congregation when an earnest evangelistic address was given. The hearty singing of more cheerful Sankey hymns interspersed with solos or other items was greatly enjoyed.

Rev John Lawrie was not a musician himself but he delighted the young folk when he introduced chorus singing. Rev James Pottinger, however, did play the organ and would bring his portable harmonium on to the scene whenever there was a need. He encouraged choir singing and got younger people involved. He was very excited when reel to reel recorders arrived in the late fifties. This was a means of taking services and music to other islands.

George Rendall, Jim Rendall, Tommy Scot , Mr Pottinger & Jack Scott.

It seemed that the Lord had set the scene for the arrival of the Rev Brydon Maben with his trombone and his singing and conducting skills. He started a Male Voice Choir that attracted men from other churches as well as the Baptists. The choir was named, "The Men of Orkney" by James McRoberts when he invited them to sing at the Glasgow Festival of Male Voice Praise in March 1961. Very soon after tapes and records were produced and sold. A similar group continues until this present day but mainly on the Orkney Mainland now.

Rev. Brydon Maben hits the low notes on his trombone.

The praise time in the Sunday services takes a more relaxed form now but is in no way less sincere. Instead of a choir and its lead, an instrumental group, of guitars and keyboards and a couple of voices on microphones will lead the singing. Michael and Teenie Harcus play a big part in this. The Harcus name appears to have had an involvement in the fellowship over the two hundred years of its existence ever since Stuart Harcus was appointed co-pastor with William Tulloch, the first minister. Michael and Teenie are following in the footsteps of these early ambassadors as they take the gospel in music and song to many places both in our own country and abroad.

Teenie & Michael Harcus pictured right at Noltland Castle

55

The choir singing in 1984, with Jim Brown leading the singing.

The platform party in 1984 singing at Jim Miller's induction:
Jimic & Jack Scott, Foster Wright, Jim Miller, Francis Gordon & Gilbert Ritchie

Gleanings from the Minutes

Rev. Griffiths came to Westray April 1901 and was authorised to procure baptismal trousers in May 1901. Many years later a minister's wife on opening the cupboard door thought she had come on a corpse when she saw the baptismal robes hanging there.

27th December 1891. George Pottinger, late of Knugdale, having accepted office in the Stromness UP Church and having given no intimation of his resignation, his name was removed from the roll. Signed: *P F Slater*

10th August1902. It was decided to accept the Rev John Hewison's (returned Baptist minister from India) offer to preach next Sunday 17th Aug, and to give the collections morning and evening to the Anglo Indian Evangelization Society of which he is an agent. Signed: *Albert Griffiths*.

December 19th1886 - At a meeting of the church today the subject of dancing was under consideration. The pastor stated that the strong feeling existing among the members signified that some action was imperative. He could not advise that any law should be made on the subject, but he asked for the sake of peace and harmony in the church those present should agree not in any way to encourage dancing in the future. This was unanimously agreed to. Signed: *P F Slater*

December 17th1905 – One month after Rev William Cramb Charteris had been inducted Murdoch Balfour, at a church meeting submitted a unanimous resolution from the diaconate proposing that the time had come when instrumental music might be introduced to the public worship to aid the praise. By January 1906 W F Brown, Breckowall had presented the church with an organ and Mrs Jane Charteris was the organist.

April 15th 1966 - The deacons wished to minute their appreciation of all that the late John Scott Drever did for the church as a Secretary (1938 – 1943), Treasurer (1941 – 1952), Deacon, Sunday School Superintendent and Church Organist.

Mrs Helen Seatter was then offered the post of organist on a permanent basis.

Mrs Helen Seatter receives a gift on her retirement as church organist in 2002

During the year it was decided to purchase a new transistor organ and have it inscribed in memory of John Drever. Mr Tim Buckley, Organising Secretary at the London Bible College and friend of the church, during a stay in Westray with his family, held a musical evening to raise funds to help pay for this organ.

Tim and Doreen Buckley, pictured left, who staged a musical evening with all four children playing their instruments.

After a visit to the church by the Peterhead Baptist Church Choir and friends, they also gave a generous donation to the organ fund. It was installed in September 1966.

Inscription on the Organ purchased to commemorate the services of John Drever

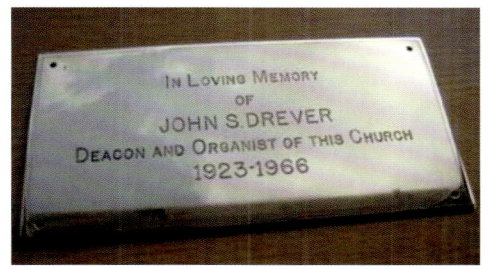

Three Generations: Duncan Drever, Anna Drever and John Drever(Junior).

For many years Cottage Meetings were arranged in different districts on a regular basis. The minister and a deacon or two deacons were appointed to conduct these meetings. They were particularly beneficial to members and friends who lived at some distance from the church and had no means of transport. People met in homes or more often in barns. The Harcuses at Swartmill, the Seatters at Newark and the Coopers at Easthill provided hospitality in the south of the island. It was noted in the minutes of the deacons meeting of Oct 1921 that there was an account for £2-15- 8d for petrol for the lamps used at cottage meetings! In the church minutes the Old School in the Westside and Peatwall and Bucklesberry in the north are also mentioned in that connection.

Since about 1960 many meetings, bible studies and latterly the weekly prayer meeting take place in private homes. WBC took a turn at holding meetings in the Eventide Home at Cleat and now United Church Gatherings meet in the Kalisgarth Care Centre at Howanbrek monthly.

8th May 1928   Mr Lawrie gave a good report of the Christian Endeavour Society highlighting how all the active members took some part in their meetings. He then handed over to the Church Treasurer the sum of £1(one pound) to the church funds, from the Christian Endeavour Society, to pay for the heating and lighting of the hall.

29th July 1929 - Mr Lawrie reported that after consultation with Mr Drever and others it was agreed to re-open the Sunday School on Sabbath 11th August and the Christian Endeavour meeting on Tuesday 6th August, as the trouble amongst the children had subsided. One wondered if there had been a water fight, popular with CE campers today or it may have been an epidemic of some childish illness though no fatalities were recorded at the time.

1930 - Tom and Ann Cooper and family, from Easthill, Skelwick, came to church firstly in a horse-drawn "spring cart" and then latterly in a "gig". The horse was stabled at Waal Cottage and given a "windling" of straw to eat. The straw had kept feet warm on the journey. Captain James Hewison of Waal Cottage and Tom Cooper served together on the diaconate for several years.

James & Nan Scott leave Berriedale for the Church Heading South

Tom & Ann Cooper, with Mary, leave Easthill for the Church heading North

1943 - It was decided to turn the manse stable into a garage to house Mr Pottinger's car. In olden times the minister had a gig with one or two ponies in order to visit out-lying homes. He could have been called out in all weathers to visit the sick and dying and also to conduct a chesting service when there was a death. We would suspect that some of the incumbents would have needed a man or boy to look after the horses and the cart.

Mr Pottinger's car had the Shetland registration PS 323. A visitor, a preacher by the name of Austin Stirling, was heard to chuckle and then say that the car was suitably labelled. He quoted Psalm 33v2 that speaks of the ten-string lyre. There was evidence of string and wire around the car!

Easter Sunday egg roll 2000. From left: Violet Drever, Ailsa Seatter, Margaret Drever, Andrew Cowan, Kirsty Hagan, Teenie Harcus, Matthew Harcus, Stuart Hagan, Hannah Harcus and Fiona Cowan

Foster's Final Fling as Rev Foster Wright leaves the service on his last Sunday

Gifts Given to the Church

In the church's early days communion wine was served from wooden cups that Rev William Tulloch had turned. One wonders if they had lasted until they were replaced by a beautiful silver service presented to the church in 1902 by Mrs David Hourston of Ayr in memory of her father Rev Henry Harcus. He had spent his last years with the Hourston family. The service consisted of two lovely silver plates and two silver goblets all decorated with the star of Bethlehem. The inscription on the one goblet says, "Presented to the Baptist Church (Westray) by Mrs David Hourston in loving memory of her father the Rev Henry Harcus pastor of the above church from1841 to1869". The Hourstons also had Orkney connections and were successful merchants in Ayr.

Cups, pictured left, given by the family of Henry Harcus

The Pulpit Bible is also a gift from Seatter Rendall, Iphs in memory of his father Seatter Rendall sen. who was a deacon in the church until his tragic death in June 1903. This was given on December 25th 1903.

Over the years many gifts including bequests, time, labour and other practical necessities for the upkeep of the sanctuary and the preaching of the gospel in Westray and elsewhere, have been generously given.

The Pulpit Bible, presented on Christmas Day1903 by the family of Seatter Rendall, see inscription below

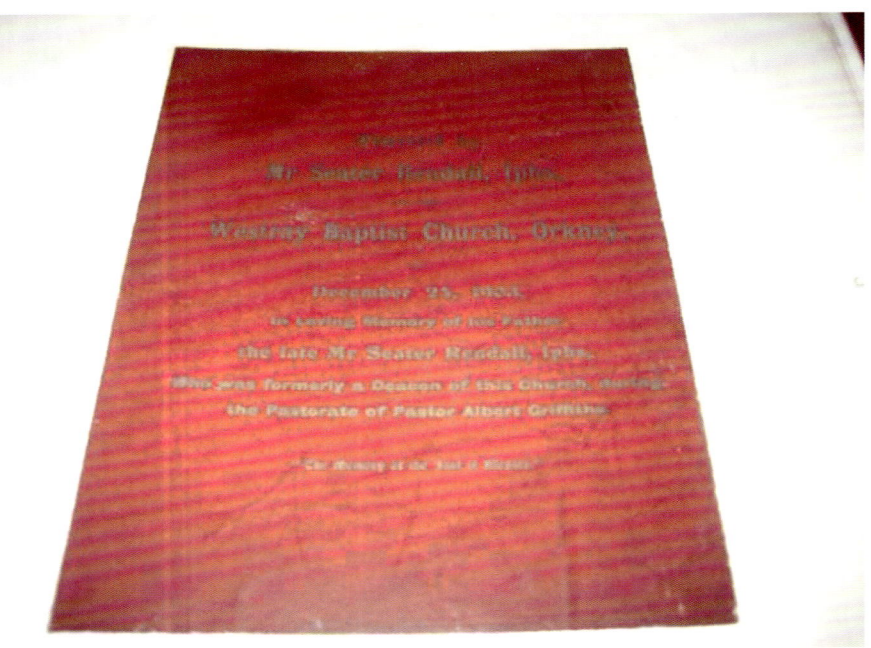

Church Life

Kirk Cleaning

The annual Kirk cleaning used to be held on a Tuesday when that was the recognised half day on the island. It started in the morning with a few folk clearing the church of books and any moveable equipment and then sweeping the floors. This gave the dust time to settle before the army of volunteers arrived after lunch with their buckets, scrubbing brushes and swabs. The same urn that boiled the water for tea on the annual social night supplied the hot water. It was mostly women that were involved in the cleaning but one of the men usually helped by climbing up a ladder to clean the high end windows and the light shades.

Back: Maggie Brown, Ada Scott, Jack Scott, Kitty Rendall, Robina Mowa,t Jessie Mowat Front: Miss Balfour, Eileen Carter, Maggie Ann Rendall, Rev. John Lawrie, Mary Rendall, Ruby Eunson, Kitty Brown.

*Back: Ruby Brown, Kit Harcus, Elsie Bain, Isabell Harcus, Margaret Rendall,
Emily Rendall, Kathleen Drever. Front: Mary Pottinger, Linda, Brenda, Rosemary
and Harry Telfer*

In later years both the Minister and the deacons have learned to
wield brooms!

*John Bain, John Harcus & Rev Jim Miller show they can sweep the cobwebs from
the sky, the Kirk and the hall respectively!*

Sundays

In the hard working lives of the island folk of the 1940s and 1950s Sunday was seen as a welcome chance to take a break and see friends and family at the Kirk. However, there were plenty of chores to attend to before the rush to get to the Kirk on time. Although the hens and pigs' tatties were boiled the night before they still had to be fed to the animals, the cows had to be milked and the general tidying up done.

There were certain things disapproved of on a Sunday – 'better never born than to have nails on Sunday shorn.' Handwork too came in for criticism. You were threatened with having to pick out the stitches with your nose on Judgement Day if you should knit or sew on the Sabbath.

Getting to the Kirk would take varying lengths of time depending on your transport. At the beginning of the 1950s there were only two cars transporting people to the Church. Mr Wm Brown, baker, and the Scotts at Skaill had cars. These were parked on the Cottage Brae and not brought into the Park. Some people came on motorbikes and perhaps a sidecar, others on push bikes, and still others brought their ponies, with or without a gig. The remainder, of course, walked.

It seems that each family had their customary seats. Skaill's seat was the back seat on the east wall. W F M Brown of Breck also sat in that seat and passed away while sitting there in 1941. The front seat on the east side in the body of the church was Carters' seat and across the middle partition sat Jeemo Bain.

Jeemo Sandison sat on the third seat on the east side. During an evening service one stormy night a gale was blowing from the east. Mr Pottinger was in the middle of his sermon when a storm blown blackbird battered on the window. A very red faced Mr Pottinger, thinking it was pranksters at the window, called out, "May the Lord rebuke thee". Jeemo smartly rose and closed the shutters. The rest of the congregation sat motionless wondering what they would find under the window when they got outside.

The Lighthouse Board paid for the lighthouse keepers to hire a taxi to take them to their chosen church once a month. However the Baptist minister used to visit the Lighthouse on a regular basis to hold a service for the staff and their families. Jeemsie drove them up collecting Kitty Brown at Noltland to play the organ they brought.

Sunday School

The Sunday School used to be held at 4.30 in the afternoon. This made getting home and then out again for the evening service at 6pm something of a rush. Some bairns made other arrangements and stayed in the village saving a trip home. Some were entertained at the Manse, others by the Drevers at the Beuith or at the home of a relative in the village while others made their own amusement which often involved pranks at the expense of others!

There was a time of choruses at the beginning with all the pupils and perhaps Bible memory verses. The boys tended to sit on the one side of the Kirk and the girls on the other. Then the Bible class went through to the Hall at the back of the Kirk, while the rest of the classes separated to various parts of the main building. In the 1940s and 1950s teachers involved were Mr Pottinger, Mrs Pottinger, John Reid of Garth, John Drever of Hewisons, Jack and Jimic Scott of Skaill. Later Tanna Drever, John Rendall of Heatherview, Molly Rendall of Berriedale, Annie Harcus of Chalmersquoy and Joy Drever from Westbreck.

Back: Linda Scott, Joy Drever, Valerie Drever, Andy Drever ,Jack Stevenson, Dave Stevenson, A. Scollay Front: Louise Drever, Margaret Scott, Fiona Scott, David Seatter, Kathleen Seatter.

It was customary for the minister to lead the Sunday School and then take the Bible Class but Jeemo Bain was superintendent at one time before John Drever succeeded him. He fulfilled this service for a long time until illness made him retire and Mr Telfer stepped in. John used the accordion to provide music for the choruses as he was able to keep an eye on the pupils. Playing the organ necessitated sitting with his back to them! Eventually John Drever's son Jeemie took over, and they started at 3pm.

Sunday School Memories by Fiona Cowan

Hid seems so very long ago, the days o' Sunday School
When we all behaved like angels and seldom broke a rule
We sat in rows in every pew, from three till nearly four,
Then home for tea, and mercy me – back tae the Kirk for more!

Jeemie was the front man standing back on to the choir
He could tell a Bible story in a way that could inspire
But then we had a memory verse we had to stand and say
If it was long and you got it wrong, try again next Sunday

The choruses were fun to sing the actions were great sport
With Christ in the vessel we all sailed into port.
We marched with the infantry, we built a house upon the rock
It was a lark, Old Noah's ark, as the people start to mock.

The boys in the back row misled us - they shouldn't have been our guide
One looked up to the boatman and said "throw me over the side!"
We gave him our "old fashioned garments", as the Jericho walls fell flat
An offering was made, a prayer was said and that was the end of that!

In recent years Sunday School and Bible Class met during the morning service. They retired to the hall, the kitchen and sometimes to a room in the manse. A crèche was provided too when it was required. Ailsa Seatter became leader when Jeemie Drever retired in 1998.

Club 3. 16 was held monthly for a time in the Community Hall where the format was more relaxed and active.

Materials and information were gathered for a time capsule which was buried in the church grounds in June 2000. Around this time, the Sunday School children performed Nativity Plays at Christmas and now join with the Parish Kirk to put on a musical annually under the guidance of Louise Harcus. Linda Hagan currently co-ordinates the children's work with many others involved in Bible Class, Sunday School and Crèche.

Youth Work

There has always been a desire to include young people in the life of the church. There was the encouragement given to them by the Pottingers, Frank Gibson with his sausage sizzles and Ken Denman with his squashes. When the Telfers came the Chippy meetings started and were very popular in the 60's and 70's. Held in the Chip Shop by kind permission of the Saintear Drevers, there was lots of singing, music and perhaps a quiz, panel or an epilogue. Jeemie and Kathleen Drever regularly had meetings for the young folk on Saturday nights at the Beuith. Stephen and Linda Hagan continued this format on Friday nights and a further Bible Study on Sunday evenings for a time in the 1980s. There were several week-ends in Papay that continued after Michael and Teenie Harcus took over in the 1990s. Trips further afield to Aberdeen were much enjoyed. Currently Louise Harcus is in charge of running the Youth Fellowship fortnightly and the Church of Scotland holding Youth Group meetings on alternate Friday evenings. The Baptist YF meetings are held in the Manse at Bellavista.

Back: Teenie, Marie, Wilma, Lisa, Mharee, Sandra & Karen Front: Michael, Wayne, Cliff, Duncan, Colin & Stephen

Picnics

In the past the annual church and Sunday School picnic was much looked forward to. A date in July was chosen and in the early days Gallowhill was the favourite site. In later years the links of Breckowall and Noltland were more popular with sometimes shelter at the Castle. The first essential was water and one of the farmers would deposit his horse-drawn water cart in the field. If the day was hot drinks of water were needed and also an abundance of tea.

On arrival everyone could have a cookie and jam and a drink of milk. During the afternoon flat races of various lengths were run by all ages and also three-legged, egg and spoon, sack and catch the train races. When it came to the actual "picnic" Brown the Baker was the man of the moment. He could heat the urn for the tea and provide the bread and teabread. Some of the women brought "duff" (clootie dumpling). When everyone was sitting around after the food a kind benefactor would toss pandrops and butter nuts around. The crowd was mobile immediately. Lots of games were then played well into the night such as rounders and freeing.

From left; first two unknown, Jack Scott, unknown lady, John Seatter and his mother Betsy of Newcastle, Betsy Scott with Jimic and Tommy Scott, George Carter, Janet Drever and Tanno Bain. Two in front are Arnold and Eileen Carter

Thanks to modern facilities a different type of picnic is regularly enjoyed these days. Outings and various rambles and barbecues can be arranged at the drop of a hat or whenever the weather forecast is right!

Back: Jeemo Bain, Mrs Pottinger, Mr Pottinger, Tanna Drever nee Bain, John S Drever, Betsy Scott nee Stout, Elbeth Leslie nee Drever, her sister Jessie Rendall nee Drever, and Johnnie Harcus. Middle: George Milne, his wife Janet nee Carter, Johnnie Scott, Mr and Mrs Reid on holiday with Margaret Drever, Ena Hewison nee Rendall Front:Elsie Gray, Gill, Annie and Margaret Drever from Papay, John Drever and Robina Davidson

Socials

Until about 1980 a Kirk Social was held annually and usually in January but the practices went on for weeks beforehand, often after the prayer meeting on a Friday night. Lots of folk can remember the excitement of turning up at a very windy Kirk hall door with fancy dresses blowing around their heads. A torch was a necessary piece of equipment on such a night, as nerves would have performers heading out the back in search of the outside toilet! The audience was handed a paper bag (pokie) as they arrived and a china cup, clammy from condensation in an unaccustomed warm church. Next followed the fun of checking to see what the bag contained. In the

50s the bag contained a piece of horse cake (black bun), a fruit square, a Paris bun and a couple of rice cakes. Later on, perhaps two sandwiches curled at the corners, one bun (queen cake), a slice of horse cake and a chocolate biscuit. From then on there would be a periodic clatter as a china cup here or there slipped off the book board and had to be caught before hitting the floor.

The Social was in two halves, the first being longer than the second. There were musical items interspersed with recitations and sketches from the Sunday school pupils. The ministers from the other Kirks each had a spot, which you hoped wasn't too long but contained plenty of funny stories! The interval was a welcome break, not just for a restorative cup of tea but because it gave the chance to stretch one's legs and indulge in a bit of light relief. The paper bags once emptied became a great source of amusement. They had a corner snipped out of them to prevent them being blown up and burst. However if the corner was pinched and twisted tightly enough then a satisfactory bang could still be achieved! Thereafter they were screwed up and fired at the nearest bald head. Occasionally they still contained scraps of sandwich or discarded bun. If they ran out of ammunition the young lads might have resorted to using pandrops which were being saved for the second half.

The water for the tea was boiled up in a big urn heated by gas. The tea was made by suspending the tealeaves in a muslin bag into the boiling water until it reached the desired colour. Generally the men were given the job of taking tea around in kettles or huge teapots. The varieties of tea offered were white, white with sugar, black and black with sugar. This saved milk and sugar having to be transported separately in what was a very crowded Kirk with little room to move around. Then came the effort of collecting up the dirty cups and debris in zinc baths, so that the rest of the Social could be enjoyed. As the night wore on the younger children got increasingly tired and eventually gave up fighting sleep. In 1950 the Baptist Social was so well received that it was repeated after a couple of weeks.

On one occasion young David Seatter could not sleep after a social. In the morning he asked why did Jack Scott sing God wanted to "take hair off you?" His mum had to explain the song was *God will take care of you* sung with a Westray accent.

Daddy o' the Manse

Mrs Pottinger had previously been a missionary in Africa and sometimes her nursing skills were called upon to help in the community or to escort an ill resident to hospital. Her widowed father came from Shetland to stay with them until his death and was called Daddy o' the Manse. When he arrived on the island it was rumoured that he had come in a drunken condition. It turned out that he had a disability that made him very unsteady on his feet. However, with grim determination he dug patches of the manse park and kept the manse in tatties and vegetables for quite a while. Mrs Pottinger always sat in the front seat at the west side of the church. She was noticed to yawn frequently throughout the sermon and her father's hearing aid would whistle periodically to the amusement of the children. This hearing aid was the first that had been seen by most folk. It consisted of a large box and a massive battery and was carried into the Church every Sunday and set on the seat beside Daddy Burgess. He sat through the whole service wearing old-fashioned earphones.

Kirk Antics

It was the custom for the young girls to sit together in the back seat on the west side of the Church, while the boys sat beside them, but separated by the central partition of wood. Any mischief the boys got up to, if witnessed by the girls, would bring sniggers of amusement from both sides of the back row.

In recent years one game played during a prayer was to roll pandrops and see how far they would travel before coming to a rest with a clatter.

Pandrops played a significant part in the church proceedings over the years. A certain gentleman was sooking a pandrop during the sermon when the sun shining in the end window made him sneeze and sent the pandrop flying!

The story goes that one of the preachers used to slip a pandrop in his mouth before starting to speak, presumably to keep his mouth moist, but it also enabled him to time his sermon. By the time the sweetie was finished it was time to sit down. However, unfortunately, once a button was popped into his mouth by mistake. We have no record of how long the sermon was that day!

Wood lice (slatos) too come in for a special mention. It was observed by three children that a slato had found its way up on to the shoulder of the gentleman in front of them. Its progress was further observed while it climbed right into his very short hairdo. Unfortunately, it tripped while climbing back down his collar and fell on the book board right under the children's noses so the youngest helped by calmly picking it up and returning it to the gentleman's shoulder.

The baptismal tank too appeared to be a favourite haunt of the slatos. One former baptismal candidate writes, 'The Chapel was full, the singing was great (led by Jim Brown who started up the chorus of the baptismal hymn as soon as each person came up from the water) but in the tank, swimming for all they were worth, were several Baptist slatos!'

Camps

Westray children became involved in the Christian Endeavour camps from the beginning. One of the first was held in 1967 in the youth hostel in north Hoy when George Rendall and Harry Telfer were the leaders. Brenda Telfer and Irene Stout were the cooks. The cooks were able to stay in the manse with the minister Rev Charles Abel. The Telfers had their two young children with them, Linda was 3 and Rosemary was still in a carrycot. The boat dropped the campers at the Moaness pier and they were ferried in turns up to the hostel by a VW van brought over to provide transport. Outings that can be recalled that year were walks to the Dwarfie Stane and up Ward hill.

Mr Telfer felt he wanted to take Westray Baptist Kirk Bible Class plus some of their friends to Dunrossness in Shetland for a camp in 1970. It was very exciting for all the campers for most had never travelled by plane before. They stayed in the Community centre and slept on mattresses kindly organised by Mr Hughes who was the minister of Dunrossness Baptist Kirk. The Bible class was asked to take part in the Sunday services at the nearby church on the Sunday.

Trips to various places were organised but the highlight was a walk to St. Ninians Isle which was reached by a stretch of sand. Zena Hutchison was the cook for the camp, helped by Elizabeth Bain. Campers included Kathleen and David Seatter, John Seatter, Linda and Margaret Scott, Margaret Bain, George Thompson, George Drever, Shirley Brown, Elizabeth Seatter, Barbara Rendall, Vicky Mears, Louise Drever and Myra Thomson.

The CE celebrated 40 years of camps in 2009 and to this day the favourite destination is Westray, which means that the Westray bairns get to travel less these days but still enjoy meeting with young people from the other isles.

Women's Work in WBC

The first women's meetings to be held in the Baptist Church, Westray as far as we know took place during Mr Charteris' pastorate. A picture taken in the church hall shows a gathering of women, one holding a young child. Relatives of the family recall that Ena Charteris was born in Westray so this may have been a forerunner of "Mothers and Toddlers". It was often said that Mrs Charteris held meetings for the Pierowall ladies of any denomination. Church minutes record that several ladies were baptised and joined the church in the last years of this ministry. Mrs Charteris quickly got involved in the newly constituted Women' Auxiliary to the Baptist Union of Scotland when they moved to the Ayr Baptist Church in 1909.

It was 1961 before Women's Auxiliary was started in Westray. Mrs Betty Maben, having been a member in Galashiels, was keen to see a branch locally and quickly organised the necessary procedures to have it inaugurated. As the National Secretary, Mrs G M Hardie, was indisposed at the time the National Treasurer, Miss A C MacFarlane, travelled to Westray and addressed a public meeting. Fortnightly meetings have continued since then with breaks during the summer. Along with the rest of Scotland the new title was adopted. WA is now known as Scottish Baptist Women's Fellowship. Most of the National Presidents have kindly visited Westray over the years. The annual social meeting when the menfolks were invited could be hilarious as some pictures show!

*Above and below the spirit of good clean fun was alive and well as the Women's
Auxiliary entertain the menfolk with a game of 'Pass the Pillowcase'*

To celebrate forty years of WA in Westray the group organised a
rally on Saturday the 8th June 2002. Lots of ladies arrived on the
ferry from Kirkwall and were whisked up to the school for breakfast.
An opportunity to visit some of Westray's tourist attractions was
given before lunch. The Celebration Rally was held in the Baptist

Kirk. Linda Hagan, Westray President, welcomed the gathering which included the National President for that time, Jan Watson, ex National Presidents Kathy Cowie and Jean McColl, Dorothy, daughter of the first Westray President, Betty Maben and Brenda Telfer, a previous local president. Kathy and Fiona McConnachie led in prayer and then Nan Scott recalled "The Beginnings of Westray WA". Isabell Harcus brought greetings from those not able to attend. Jean McColl led the praise time, Brenda did a reading and Jan gave an inspiring address. The local ladies put on a musical item and also a play after the fashion of early meetings when the ladies met to help each other such as on a hen plucking night! After these proceedings a lovely tea with sandwiches and cakes was served.

Back: Isabell Harcus, Brenda Telfer, Fiona MacConnachie, Linda Hagan
Front: Cathy Cowie, Jan Watson & Jean McColl

The hospitality in Westray is always very generous and another similar event hosted by Westray ladies took place in June 2008 when they invited Reona Petersen Joly to come and tell of her amazing and dangerous experiences as she worked in Albania. Christians were not welcome in Communist Albania in the 1970s. About eighty ladies, and three men in the music group, were touched with the enthralling stories she had to tell. The Mustard Seed was there and sold many of her books, "*Tomorrow We Die*".

Angela, Julie, Cheryl & Louise who planned the event with Reona Peterson Joly

Westray can boast to have had three ministers' wives who have been National Presidents of Scottish Baptist Women's Fellowship or WA Jean McColl was in that position before she came to Westray and Jean Wright and Fiona MacConnachie after they left.

Women's Fellowship is currently run by a committee and several ladies share the leadership. They continue to meet fortnightly and also join with the Church of Scotland for World Day of Prayer and Christmas events. They support Tear Fund's Children at Risk Programme financially and as a group they continue to support the church practically with hospitality, cleaning and decorating. The SBWF motto continues to be 'Serving God in everything'.

Pioneers

Mrs Pottinger worked in Luampa in Africa with the South Africa General Mission and while in Westray she set up a support group for the Mission. The aim was to find out about the missionaries, pray for them and make articles of clothes or blankets that they could distribute to needy folk. This group was called the Pioneers and met initially in an upstairs room in the manse. While the girls were involved in this very practical work Mr Pottinger took the boys for woodwork and other handwork in the garage. He had been trained as a joiner and together they mended organs and made boxes and other small items.

In addition to knitting squares for blankets, dresses were sewn for girls from a simple pattern, and all were of orange fabric from a large bale. Some of the pioneers were surprised to learn the reason the dresses were all the same was that it was school uniforms they had been sewing.

For many years after the Pottingers left Annie Harcus carried on the work with the young folk. The boys still came along to join in the fun and some of them even learned to knit! Alice Rendall helped while she lived in Westray along with Rene Berstan, Alison Pottinger and Ruth Bain as did some of the ministers' wives. The pioneers continued for 40 plus years until very recently the very small number of girls and the changing missionary scene saw the faithful group disband.

Christian Endeavour

During the year, the CE met on a Friday night in the back hall at the Kirk. The hall always felt full and there was a number of young folk who didn't regularly come to the Kirk. Singing was always a favourite, with Kathleen Seatter on the organ and Duncan Drever playing the guitar. The 'action' choruses were a hit, especially 'I may never march with the infantry' 'I'm inright, outright, upright, downright, happy all the time' and 'In my Father's house.'

Highlights of the CE year were the Christmas party and CE camp. The Christmas party was held in St. George's Hall in the village. There was always plenty of games and food but the main event was 'duster hockey.' This involved using two walking sticks upside down as our hockey sticks to hit a knotted duster! Although I'm sure it wasn't meant to be a violent game, due to the competitive spirit there were usually a few bruises to show off the next day! CE camp used to run for three weeks, with a junior, intermediate and senior camp. Camp has played a very significant part in many Orkney young folk's spiritual walk. It was always a time to learn more about God and really focus on what He was saying to you. A number of Westray young folk have given their lives to God over these weeks. Highlights of the camp week were the sports day, the water fight, the concert on the last night and waking up on the last day to see what mischief the leaders had done to the campers.....over the years we had campers waking up in fields, being tied together or wearing make-up!

What made Westray CE special was having the leadership of Jeemie Drever. He was a godly man who was committed to teaching and showing the young folk Jesus but also someone who enjoyed having fun and had a great sense of humour! I know that he played a very significant part in helping many of the young people on Westray grow in their understanding and faith in God.

Mission Teams

Over the years several groups have volunteered to help the Westray Baptist Church in practical ways and in spiritual ways. In 1964 Tom Scott, from Howe, Harray was one of a team of Edinburgh Baptist students who formed a work party that volunteered to help. They were under the leadership of Ian McKinlay. The boys blamed the girls for a couple of mishaps, paint spilt on the pews and a pane of glass coming into the church quickly followed by a bucket of water! After a fortnight they left the church redecorated outside and inside. It was no mean task that they had undertaken and the fact that the plaster and pebble dashing stands intact to this day proves they did good job.

The first EBSA mission team repair the harling in 1964 – good job!

81

CHRIST IS THE ANSWER

Campaign at
THE BAPTIST CHURCH
WESTRAY

Carolyn Duncan
Freda Anthony
Anne Russell
Trix Bulten
Moira Leslie

May 21st - June 12th

In June 1966 a team of WEC students held a campaign at the church. The group consisted of five girls, from England, Scotland, Ireland and Holland, who held meetings for four weeks. They were well received and some have kept in contact over the years. Friendships were renewed when Fiona Scott met Moira Leslie when she recently applied to join WEC. Some of the young converts then began a group in the school at lunchtimes. Margaret Scott and Anne Seatter led the group, and so the outreach continued.

In 1979 another team of Edinburgh Baptist Student Association (EBSA) students were summoned to arrange a holiday Club for August, one week in Westray the next in Sanday.

The team had a great week of meetings in the Church and in the Chip Shop as well as a film night in St George's Hall. There was a sea drama at the North Banks and one of the team had to haul Fiona Scott out of a rip tide. This started a bit of romance and when Les Cowan, a member of the team, left Orkney the following Friday an engagement between them had been agreed.

The Scottish Baptist News of October 1979 had the following item along with a picture of Jack Scott and his Rallye plane.

Flying start for Orkney Mission

"During August Rev Foster Wright of the Westray Baptist Church, together with a team of four students from Edinburgh engaged in extensive visitation on the island of Sanday, covering 100 homes of the 160 homes there. Their means of transport on the outward journey was a small plane which is the property of the church secretary in Westray, and they made the return journey by boat.

Mr Wright reports that the reception to the visitation was extremely favourable and that a rally which was held on the Thursday evening of the week of visitation, at which men from the Westray Church came to sing, had an attendance of 60. Following the meeting many expressions of appreciation were received.

The next stage of this outreach will be during November when the Westray Church has released their minister to spend a month on the island where he has secured the use of a cottage. He will be accompanied during that time by a colleague from Wales who has been a worker with the "Youth for Christ" organisation."

Back: Alan Berry, Jack Scott Middle:Foster Wright, Pam, Jacqui,Gilbert Ritchie Front: Ann Berry(with Children standing) Heather, Lesley(holding Rebekah) Fiona and Les on the mission team of 1980 on the deck of the Coriander.

During Mr Wright's ministry in Westray several evangelistic visits were made to Sanday. A caravan sited at the Sanday Baptist Church was the accommodation.

Alan Berry, Founder of the Bethany Trust remembers these days.

'As a family we first met Foster Wright when we gave him hospitality while he was a delegate from the Westray Church at the Baptist Assembly. I then visited Westray in my capacity as President of Christian Endeavour and the two families decided to exchange pulpits and manses for holidays. For us it was idyllic - no traffic for the children to worry about as they careered around on bikes and were delighted that the Browns named a calf and a kitten after them; wonderful deserted beaches to explore; having fun dressing up in wet suits; gleaning a little of Nan Scott's ornithological expertise; trips in Jack's plane and catching mackerel with Duncan Drever, and not forgetting the time we tried to row against the tide in Pierowall Bay and had the folks at the bakery and half the island on red alert! Then there was Jack's kindness in leaving Pierowall at 4.00am to take us to Kirkwall in the *Coriander* so that we could be back in Edinburgh in time to take a funeral.

Two missions on Sanday were also memorable. We used the church building and vestry and a caravan for accommodation, with Mrs. Work next door to the church kindly letting us use her shower. Part of the group caused great consternation on the small ferry from John O' Groats as they were accompanied by just about everything but the kitchen sink, including a fridge! The caravan was purchased in Fife and towed all the way to the ferry with Rev Bill Cowie acting as my intrepid co-driver. Going up and down the Berriedale Braes pulling a 22ft. caravan was an experience I wouldn't like to repeat. We also had an old Mazda with which we went round Sanday collecting children for the daytime activities. The condition of its exhaust meant that everyone knew it was coming miles before it came into view. As well as getting plenty of exercise visiting homes spread out over the south of the island, the team were involved in evening meetings for adults and Sunday services. It was wonderful to see the old building being used for worship again. Team members mainly came from Scottish Baptist Churches, but the second year two teenagers from Belgium and a Nigerian doctor who was studying in Edinburgh joined us. That year too we benefited from the experience and enthusiasm of retired B.M.S. missionary Winnie Haddon and her ukulele and when the visiting preacher on

Westray took ill some of the team had the privilege of going across the water to take the Westray evening service The missions were learning experiences and fun and fellowship for the teams and times of sowing God's Word, which we trust will have borne fruit in the lives of those who heard.'

Then in August 1986 a group of young people, seven boys and seven girls, friends of Carol Drever, from Queen's Park Baptist Church, Glasgow came for a holiday. They asked for accommodation in the church. That worked very well. Some took part in an open evangelistic meeting on the Friday and in the Sunday services. They also organised games for the young folk. For some it became a romantic experience and Heather and John Bath announced their engagement one night they were all asked out to tea. Two other couples that married later on were Ivy and Tam Young and June and Graham Cameron. Again, there must have been something in the air.

There certainly was 'something in the air' at the former Manse when the Kitchen roof was raised during renovations

Congratulations to Davie & Maggie Burgher on their 70th Wedding Anniversary from Rev Gilbert Ritchie, President of the Baptist Union of Scotland

Rev. Jim Miller presents a Barometer to Jack and Nan Scott when Jack retired after 43 years as church secretary.

Missionary Interests

Ever since its constitution WBC has always had a desire to spread the gospel to others. We read that during the first fifty years of its existence there had even been an interest in Foreign Missions. John Reid left bequests to the **Home Baptist Missionary Society of Scotland**, the **English Strict Baptist Society**, the **London Foreign Baptist Missionary Society** and the **German Baptist Society on** his death in1865.

The first minister William Tulloch missioned through some other Orkney islands and two co- pastors, Robert Seatter and Stewart Harcus were appointed to do the pulpit work in his absence. As the years went on other pastors went on to preach in Eday and Sanday and sometimes in Burray. The Orkney Baptist Missionary Society was founded in 1849 in order to administer funds for the Baptist work in the islands. Rev Henry Harcus and Rev James Scott were two of the first to be helped. Meetings were held annually in different islands when reports of the work in Orkney were given, someone would give an address and then there was prayer for the continuing evangelisation of Orkney. The Society wound up its operations in 1968 since Westray had been going it alone since the early fifties. The churches in Sanday and Eday were closed in 1954. However before that several Westray members enjoyed a memorable meeting in Eday travelling from Rapness to Eday in a very full small fishing boat! Pastor William and Mrs Dora Tregunna made excellent hosts. Mr Pottinger, Westray minister, and Rev Jim Thomson were in the Westray party. At the end of the meeting the chairman asked for a favourite closing hymn. Sitting in a back seat Jim Thomson called for "Blest be the tie that binds" and at the same time he was busy tying the coat belt of the man in front to his chair. Such was Jim's humour.

Through the **Baptist Missionary Society** a long relationship with an indigenous evangelist, Albert Padhan, was formed. Lots of letters were exchanged over the years and it is probably thanks to Violet Drever and her father before her that some of these letters from as far back as 1909 survive, with stamps on some still intact. Violet's father, W F M Brown was appointed collector and auditor for the Padhan Fund in 1938. The interest in India may have started when Rev John R Hewison, Pierowall Westray, missioned in India for a time with the Salvation Army around 1905.

The minutes show that in 1909 the following deacons were serving when the receipt of £3, "The balance of the first year's salary for native Evangelist in India was acknowledged" by the Baptist Missionary Society. The support for this man, Babu Albert Padhan was still ongoing in 1938.

Many letters were exchanged over the years and he sent a picture of himself and his family. He also requested a picture of his benefactors. We think this was the reason for this photograph. We also think the photographer was the renowned Tom Kent but perhaps not his best reproduction!

Back : Captain John Craigie, John Tulloch, James Scott, David Thomson and W F Brown Front: Captain James Hewison, Rev William C Charteris, David Drever and Murdoch Balfour. (Signatures for the above are found on page 28.)

Albert Padhan with wife and baby born January 1909

Page One of Albert Padhan's letter to Westray Baptist Church
(See translation on next page – if required!)

Translation of Babu Albert Padhan's Letter

Aska, Ganjam.
18/9/10.

Dear Brethren,

Last December I sent you a letter, but I am sorry to hear that you did not receive it. I was transferred here last year.

Up to the present there is no Church here. A few (Christian) people are residing here on account of their work. The number is not large. As we have no Chapel we worship in the house of the various friends.

Most of the people of the place are Hindus, and they are our nearest neighbours.
We have had no opportunity as yet to send you our photo, and we are sorry (for the omission) nevertheless we shall be very glad to see your photo if you can do us the favour to send it.

Last January we had a little daughter born to us.

Yesterday afternoon as I was going to preach in a village a man on the road asked me what work I was doing. I told him my work was to make known the religion of Jesus Christ, and I asked him "Do you know anything of this religion?" "Yes" he said, "It is the true religion". So I went on to tell him that if it were the true religion he should not merely say so but should embrace it, otherwise there was no advantage in his assertion. He then said, "It is gradually spreading and at last all will accept it." We find from experience that this opinion is gaining ground day by day. We believe that the Lord will speedily bring the day to pass when India shall be His, and He shall be the Saviour whom all shall know.

Next month we are going out on tour to do the Lord's work. Pray that as we do it we may see the fruit of our labours, and be preserved in health so that we may accomplish it satisfactorily.

Finally accept our salutations.

(I remain) One ever desiring a place in your love

Albert Padhan.

Missions and Missionaries that WBC has supported over the years.

Geoffrey Payne working with the **South African General Mission** often visited the church in the nineteen fifties. This was the Mission that Helen Pottinger worked with before she married. Poor Geoffrey was to conduct a cottage meeting at Skaill one stormy night when Mr Pottinger closed the car door on his finger. After some first aid he bravely carried on Because of these connections a Pioneer group was set up for the girls in the church. Mrs Pottinger and Annie Harcus, Chalmersquoy led this group very successfully for many years. The girls got news of the mission from visitors and from letters and they made and collected things to send to the missionaries. The WA too sent many parcels to the Mission at Luampa. Every fourth WA meeting was a knitting night or a night to make up parcels. Some years after Mr Pottinger died Mrs Pottinger returned to the station where she had worked in Africa. After she got back to Shetland, where they had retired, she visited the Westray Church and gave a report on the warm welcome that she had got and how she had been able to help with the work. She also spent some time as the district nurse on Fair Isle during her retirement.

For many years Ruby Eunson was the representative for the **Leprosy Mission.**

Jim and Mollie Fleming from Larbert Baptist Church, working with **Africa Evangelical Fellowship** 1980 – 1990 in Gwanda, Zimbabwe and then in the book-shop in Harare, Zimbabwe.

Kenneth and Jeannie Scott working with **Regions Beyond Missionary Union (now part of Latin Link**) 1973 – 1991. They were led to work in South America first in Apurimac, Peru and then in Lima. Although Kenneth had been a member of Kirkwall Baptist Church he was actually a kinsman of the Rev James Scott of Keiss and Canisbay fame both being descended from a Scott of Trenabie. Miss Jemima Carter organised Westray's support for Kenneth.

Foster and Jean Wright in Zaire approx 1987-1991 with the **Baptist Missionary Society**. And more recently Angus and Carol MacNeill in Thailand and Steve and Jane Williams, whilst in Cyprus.

Eddie and Rosemary Watt in Kenya with the **Missionary Aviation Fellowship**.

In August 2007 Julie Hagan, a member of Westray Baptist Church, went out to work as a youth worker at St Columba's Presbyterian Church in Mutare, Zimbabwe after spending four months there in 2005 while she was volunteering for a year with **Oasis Trust**. Unemployment in Zimbabwe is around 95% and Julie was particularly aware that there are so few opportunities for women. She felt God gave her a vision to start an income generating project for ladies using her experience in Africa and the craft skills she had grown up with in Westray, especially working at Hume Sweet Hume.

She started the project with 6 women, 3 were women from a Child Protection Program and 3 were officers from the local prison. The officers in turn taught the female inmates and so it became part of the rehabilitation plan. Since it started, **Gogo Olive**, as the charity is now known, has expanded to support 50 women.

The idea was to knit safari animals. Knitting was chosen as it only requires basic materials, can be done anywhere and at any time which suits the lifestyle of African women. Knitting and selling the animals gives the women something to focus on and allows them to support their families. Julie and her team visit the prison on a weekly basis and have a time of fellowship, prayer and worship as well as bringing refreshments. Julie says that it is amazing to see the change in the women's lives when they are offered hope, and God's love is shown to them in practical ways.

Julie is excited about future developments as her sister Ruth is going to join her in Zimbabwe. Both girls are grateful for the foundation in faith they received in the Westray Baptist Church and for the support they continue to get from the church

The women's auxiliary have always great supporters of mission by knitting. Pictured here: Back: Ivy Stout (visiting), Elma Brown, Ruby Rendall, Kathleen Drever & Helen Seatter Middle: Mary Pottinger, Ruby Brown, Elsie Bain, Georgina Rendall, Front: Ruby Eunson ,Cathy Cowie (National WA President) Kitty Brown and Tanno Drever

And a new style of missionary endeavour as Julie Hagan passes on Westray knitting skills for self support in Zimbabwe through the project Gogo Olive.

Feth Ga'an Forrard

By Annie Harcus

Lang geen bi, a group o' fok
Met taegither, whit ither bit tae gab? Sum gawk'd
I suppose hid wis draftee ae the room.
Guess whie? Portholes wi nee gless, fraish air atween them an the moon.

Noutlan Castle standin therr fur Mary Queen o' Scots.
Whie no yuse hid? Biggin kirks dus kost a fang.
Fairly sizeable, hid wad haad a dizzen or twa
Livvin buddies wi souls, an dressd in thir Sunday best, lukkin reall braw.

Hid was a gathrin o' souls wantin fellowship
Aroond God's wurd, wi fok they kent.
The Bible dus sae hids an important thing
Tae gather taegithir ae the companie o' a King.

Eftir a whyle hid wis aa plann'd
Tae bild a kirk, an caa a man
Fur tae be meenistir fuul time, an bide at a manse
Oo my, whit next? Will wae grab this chance?

Annie ' the peedie poet'

Beuys, hid wis ae idea fae a hihir pooer
Wae oot a doot, sum fok wid gossip, an glower.
"Relegous daffties," war in tuuch wi a Winderful freend,
An shawed the island that thae hed feth an wir keen.

Thro the years, wae've seen many things happenin here.
Bible class, Sunday skeull, Christian Endeavour, Pioneers, Male Voice
Choir etc, the Lord's neem revered.
Prayer meetins arr challenging, an can be livelee occasions,
Bit verrie important, wioot them there can be divershuns.

Wan nite a veesitor cam intae the hall, lukkin for fun
He flixd bent heid'd weemen, so thae climmerd aff the grund
Ap on thae saets, an screekd virrie lood.
The moose wis irreverent, an he didno' care a hoot.

In deys o' yore, wan meenister an guid wife wir affy kind
Helpd aabuddy, no metter whither sited or blind.
Thae own'd a rare vehicle which wis caad "Shekina Box" an hid shuck
roond the bends, bangd, an crackd,
while passengirs winderd if this wis neer thir end.

Anither hed Aikerness "holmey" sheep
Tetherid ae the manse perk, tae aet gress an weeds
Posh grub instead o' bein want wi tangle satt.
Thea thrivd ower weel, still wari o' ordinari fok.

Buzz, an Calvin, twa furry fower leggd freens.
Wir keen tae cum tae lissen, whin the sermon wis been.
Thae kent sum fok that warno keen
Tae see thim, whin thae wir ment tae be heem.

May God bliss this kirk in future days
Wae gae Him thanks, wi prayer an' praise.
Welcum tae ivirie bodie that cums thro the door
An' hope yu'll cum again, the Lord tae adore.

Thanks to Annie for her inspirational poem, written in her own
Westray dialect and summing up our sentiments about our home
church.

Indeed we give God thanks for the history in which we have all
shared and look to Him for blessings in future days – by 'faith going
forward'.

Further Reading

The History of the Orkney Baptist Churches by Rev Henry Harcus

The lives of Robert and James Haldane by Alexander Haldane

History of the Baptists in Scotland edited by Rev George Yuille

Thirty years a Colporteur by Thomas Groat

The Baptists in Scotland, a History edited by D W Bebbington

The First 100years of the BU of Scotland by Rev Derek B Murray

Glory in the Glen by Tom Lennie

Lerwick Baptist Church History by John A Leslie

Westray Baptist Church Newsletters

Scottish Baptist Yearbooks, Reports

Scottish Baptist News

Days of Orkney Steam by Alastair & Anne Cormack

"*Evangelist*" a magazine published from1846-1853

On Holy Ground by Iain MacDonald & Others

The New Kirk in Westray by Nancy Scott

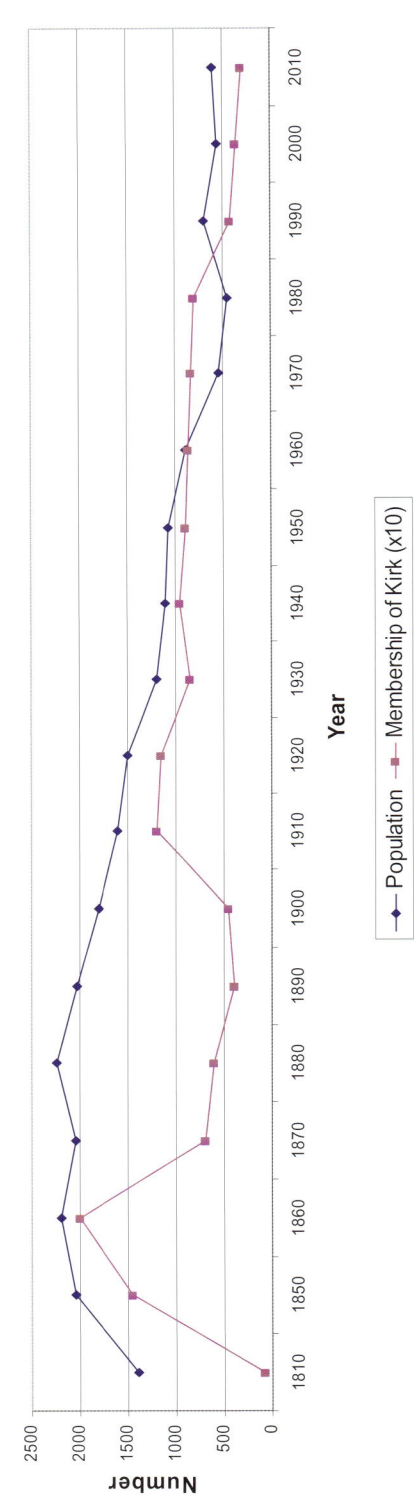

Westray population vs Kirk members

Ministers

William Tulloch	1810 – 1858
Henry Harcus	1843 – 1868
George Macdonald	1870 – 1875
J. A. Marnie	1879 – 1881
P. F. Slater	1881 – 1894
J. Yeomans	1895 – 1900
A. Griffiths	1901 – 1905
W. C. Charteris	1905 – 1909
William Gilmour	1909 – 1916
Edward Hogg	1916 – 1927
John Lawrie	1927 – 1942
James Pottinger	1942 – 1959
Kenneth Denman	*1959 – 1960*
Brydon Maben	1960 – 1963
Henry R Telfer	1963 – 1970
Raymond Thomson	1971 – 1977
Foster C Wright	1977 – 1983
James Miller	1983 – 1989
Archie McColl	1990 – 1995
Hugh McConnachie	1996 – 2001
Stephen Langford	2002 – 2006
Gavin Hunter	2010 –

Deacons in 1984. Back: John Drever, Billy Brown, Jeemie Drever
Middle: Gavin Seatter, Jack Scott, John Bain
Front Davie Burgher, Rev Jim Miller and HarryRendall

Deacons in 2010 :Michael Harcus, Stephen Hagan, George Thomson,
John Drever & John Harcus

Deacons

Originally deacons were appointed and were not expected to resign so there is no list of how long each deacon was in office. There is however some dates of appointments. The first list we have is from legal papers written in 1861. Other dates given are just an indication of when the accompanying names were in office.

1861 Thomas Harcus, carpenter, Voldigar
   James Harcus, farmer, Swartmill
   Peter Harcus, Ground Officer, East Voldigar
   Matthew Harcus, blacksmith/farmer, Mid Ouseness
   John Hewison, merchant, Beuth
   Murdoch Hewison, shopman, Grindlay
   William Scott, farmer, Tuquoy
   Thomas Logie, Farm manager, Skaill
   William Reid, Blacksmith, Rebuilding

1889 John Reid and
   William Pottinger, Knugdale,(both signed the minutes as deacons)

1891 David Drever, Links
   Henry Drever, Pierowall
   William Reid

1894 John Tulloch

1901 Seatter Rendall, Iphs
   William Frederick M Brown, baker/farmer, Gill Pier/ Breckowall
   James Scott, farmer, Gill/Vestry
   Murdoch Balfour, Chalmersquoy

1908 Captain John Craigie, Sea Captain, 4 Gill Pier
   David Drever, farmer, Links
   Captain James Hewison, merchant, Pierowall/Waal Cottage

James Scott, farmer, Gill/Vestry
David Thomson, fisherman, Links then Fueld
John Tulloch, fisherman, Links

1912   John Drever at Gill
Thomas Bain, Links

1917   Thomas Cooper, Easthill
James Sandison, Pierowall

1919   James Bain, Broughton

1930   Sinclair Rendall, Ring

1937   David Burgher, Cubbigeo
Sinclair Cooper, Easthill

1941   John Reid, Garth
John Scott, jun, Skaill

1944   George Rendall, jun, Berriedale
Tom Scott, Skaill

1955   John Seatter, Newcastle

1961   Gavin Seatter, Links
William F Brown, Noltland
William Drever, Westbreck

1962   John Bain, Broughton
Henry Rendall, Bucklesberry
James Drever, Beuith

1985   John Drever, 3 Gill Pier

1988   Stephen Hagan, Skaill
John Harcus, Chalmersquoy
David Seatter, Tirlot

2000   George Thomson. Midouseness
Michael Harcus, Rosevale, Pierowall

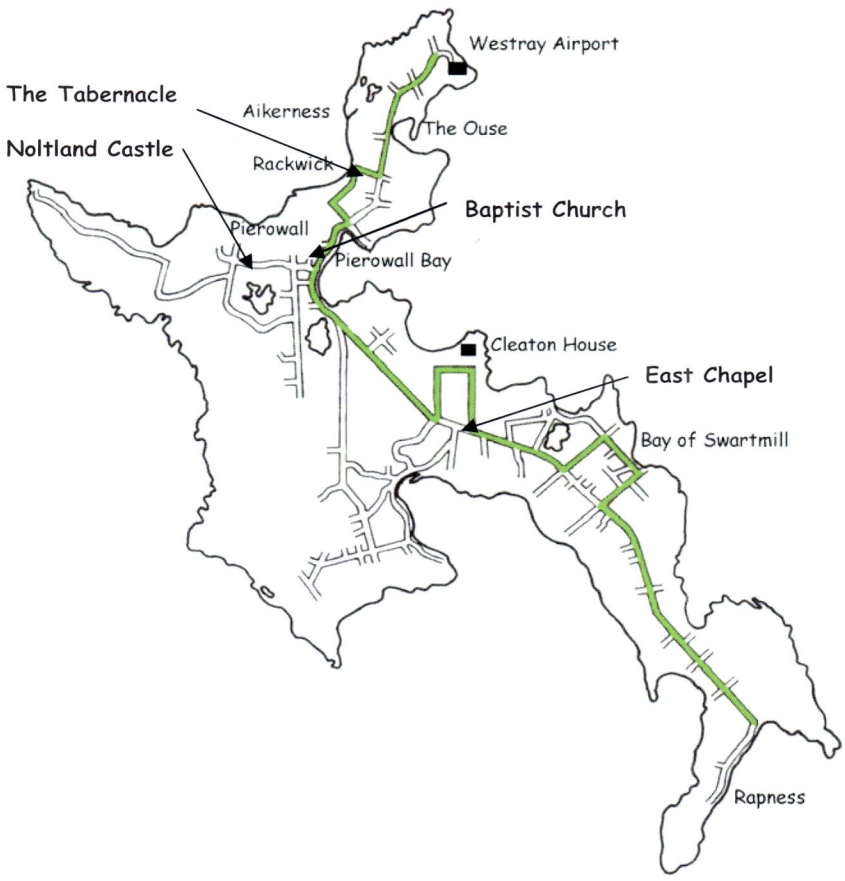

The Tabernacle

Noltland Castle

Westray Airport

Aikerness

The Ouse

Rackwick

Baptist Church

Pierowall

Pierowall Bay

Cleaton House

East Chapel

Bay of Swartmill

Rapness

Cover images: Top: Westray Baptist Kirk, present meeting place

Bottom (left to right): Noltland Castle, early meeting place.

East Chapel, meeting place in use from 1839

Site of 'The Tabernacle' meeting place until 1850